IT'S THE GREATEST DAY YOU EVER LIVED

It's the Greatest Day You Ever Lived

DON DOUBLE

KINGSWAY PUBLICATIONS
EASTBOURNE

Copyright © Don Double 1988

First published 1988

All rights reserved.
No part of this publication may be reproduced or
transmitted in any form or by any means, electronic
or mechanical, including photocopy, recording, or any
information storage and retrieval system, without
permission in writing from the publisher.

Most biblical quotations are from the Revised Authorised
Version © Thomas Nelson Inc. 1982. Use is also made of
the Authorised Version, Crown copyright; the Jerusalem
Bible © Darton, Longman and Todd Ltd and Doubleday & Co,
1966, 1967, 1968; the Amplified Bible, OT © Zondervan
Publishing House 1962, 1964, NT © Lockman Foundation
1954, 1958; New International Version © International
Bible Society 1973, 1978, 1984, published by Hodder &
Stoughton; and the New American Standard Bible © The
Lockman Foundation 1960, 1962, 1963, 1968, 1971, 1972, 1973.

Cover photo: Tony Stone Photolibrary—London

British Library Cataloguing in Publication Data

Double, Don, *1934—*
  It's the greatest day you ever lived.
  1. Christian life
  I. Title
  248.4

ISBN 0-86065-609-8

Produced and printed in Great Britain for
KINGSWAY PUBLICATIONS LTD
Lottbridge Drove, Eastbourne, E Sussex BN23 6NT by
Nuprint Ltd, Harpenden, Herts AL5 4SE

*To all those who desire to live in
the fullness of all that God has
for them, and thus to have a
great day every day.*

Contents

	Acknowledgements	9
1.	Have a Great Day	11
2.	Don't Settle for Less Than God's Best	27
3.	The Book with God in It	43
4.	Hearing from Heaven	55
5.	It Moved	67
6.	How to Walk on Water	77
7.	Fear Sees Ghosts—Faith Sees Jesus	95
8.	I'm a Blessing Everywhere I Go	107
9.	Poverty Is Not a Virtue	123
10.	The Good Life	141

Acknowledgements

Thanks to Mike Darwood for his part in the writing of this book. Thanks also to Andrea Hughes for her hard work typing it into the word processor, to Brian and Iris Powell, Clare Telfer, Vicky Hughes, Pat Darwood and Carol Mettrick for proof-reading, and to various other members of my team who helped to get the book out on time.

1. Have a Great Day

'Have a nice day,' said the shop assistant as I pocketed my change, picked up my purchase, and turned to the door. Whether she meant it or not, the pretty girl with her flashing smile and attractive voice certainly left a good impression on me. As I left the shop, I thought of one of my favourite sayings: 'It's the greatest day you've ever lived.' I always say that in faith because I am convinced that for the Christian every day can be a great day, even if the person I am speaking to feels that so far their day has been an unmitigated disaster. It is my goal that this book will help you to discover the secret of having a great day—every day.

When I became a Christian over thirty years ago, I began to read God's word and put it into practice. During that time, I discovered some essential ingredients of a great day and I would like to share this recipe with you. Put it into practice and I believe you will be as pleased with it as I am.

What is a great day? No doubt you will have your own ideas on how to answer that question, but, for the Christian, it will certainly include living in victory over sin of all kinds, including the doubts, worries and unbelief that lead so many Christians into depressions. It will be a day in which we are continually being filled with the Holy Spirit and walking in step with him. We shall go about with a glad heart, rejoicing in the goodness of God and enjoying his abundant provision. All through the day, we shall be glad to be alive and as it draws to a close we shall feel fulfilled and free from condemnation. There will also be the satisfaction of knowing that the devil has been having a hard time with us, and that we have spent the day in the will of God.

You might think that my description of a great day is wishful thinking, something that you could never achieve, but I believe that it is God's normal standard for every Christian. The secret of success is to accept that standard as your goal and aim for it. Until you do that there will be no progress towards it in your life.

On one occasion, when I was staying with the Principal of a Bible College, we went to a meeting together one evening and as we were walking home afterwards I asked him what he thought about the meeting. I have never forgotten his reply: 'Well, to tell you the truth, I think that they aimed at nothing and hit it. They scored a bullseye.' Christians without goals wander aimlessly and get more and more frustrated as time passes. As you get to know God's will for your life and make it your goal to be in his will, you will have a target for a great day to aim at. Then go for it with everything you have. That way you will find that every day is better than the day before, and the greatest day that you ever lived!

In his first letter to the Corinthians, Paul uses the illustration of an athlete training for the Olympic Games (1 Cor 9:24–27). It is a picture of a man under a self-imposed, rigorous and strictly disciplined regime of training. The athlete has a clear goal, and that is to win his race. To achieve this aim, he brings his body into subjection, putting his heart and soul into his training over a sustained period of time, driving himself to a peak of fitness as the day of the race approaches.

A modern-day Olympic athlete is not aiming for a bronze medal, or even a silver one. He has set his heart on the first prize, and is 'going for gold'. The Christian should take the athlete as his example and be equally dedicated to being a winner and living a victorious Christian life every day.

I am sure that one of the main reasons why so many Christians experience failure and condemnation is because they do not have a clear vision of the victorious life of faith as their goal. Negative preaching and a general atmosphere of unbelief are largely responsible for this. As the Bible puts it, 'Where there is no vision, the people perish (Prov 29:18, AV). As a boy, I was a keen cyclist, and I became quite an expert at mending punctures. When I had a nice new tyre and inner tube that was quite easy, but as they got older I had more trouble mending the tube until I finally decided that it had perished and was no longer of any use for the purpose for which it had been made. It was still there but useless and ineffective. In the same way, an aimless Christian will experience defeat, discouragement, depression and failure. He will have a miserable life, being of no use to himself or anyone else, and bringing no glory to God.

If we have a vision of God's will and plan for our lives and let it become our motivating force, then however far we are from its fulfilment, we shall be going in the right direction. The confidence that we are going the right way will in itself help us to move

IT'S THE GREATEST DAY YOU EVER LIVED

faster. Then remember that God has provided you with everything you need for godly living (2 Pet 1:3) and go for gold, because in the kingdom of God you can be a gold medalist *every day!* Believe that it is possible, expect it to happen and every day will be great.

In his letter to the Philippians, we see Paul going for gold. He starts with a prayer: 'That I may know him and the power of his resurrection, and the fellowship of his sufferings, being conformed to his death, if, by any means, I may attain to the resurrection from the dead' (Phil 3:10–11). In this, he is expressing his desire to God and sharing his vision with him. His following words are: 'I press towards the goal for the prize of the upward call of God in Christ Jesus' (Phil 3:14). He is saying in other words, 'I am going for a gold medal.' For the athlete, the medal has an impression stamped on it. The victorious Christian bears on his body the stamp of the Lord Jesus Christ. He becomes like him. We should be motivated by a burning desire to be like Jesus, every day.

Every business does a stocktaking at least once every year, and I understand that the more progressive and competitive firms take stock much more frequently than that, sometimes as often as once every month! I believe that we too should take stock of our lives on a regular basis, asking ourselves the question, 'Am I more like Jesus than I was a month ago?' Picture yourself a spectator at the Olympic Games watching the contestants line up for the 100 metres race. One man is dressed in wellington boots, a heavy overcoat and scarf, and a woolly hat. The rest are wearing shorts, singlets and running shoes. You might well feel confident that you could point out one man who is not going to win the race! The sensible athlete is careful not to carry any excess weight. In the same way, the Christian is exhorted to 'lay aside every weight, and the sin which so easily ensnares us, and let us run with endurance the race that is set before us' (Heb 12:1).

I have heard a number of sermons on the subject of the sin that clings so closely to us or, as the Authorised Version puts it, 'the sin which doth so easily beset us' (Heb 12:1), and all the preachers had their own ideas about the besetting sin. I believe it is vital that we consider a verse of Scripture in its context and the context of that verse is faith. This leads me to the conclusion that the besetting sin is unbelief. It is certainly one we all have problems with.

The book of Hebrews has a lot to say about faith and unbelief, and it reminds us that the Israelites who came out of Egypt with Moses did not enter the promised land 'because of unbelief' (Heb 3:19). I fear that there is a lot of negative preaching in the churches today that fosters unbelief and hinders us from reaching the quality of life that God has made available to us. Some sermons are no more than a load of excuses for living a sub-standard Christian life, and the lives of both the preacher and congregation provide an illustration of the scripture: 'Whatever a man sows, that he will also reap' (Gal 6:7). Some Christians positively enjoy listening to such negative preaching because it justifies their lack of progress in the Christian life and enables them to settle for less than God's best without feeling uncomfortable about it. Negative preaching produces unbelief and a crop of poor fruit in the lives of those who receive it.

I have discovered nine keys to having a great day

that can unlock the door of your prison and set you free to enjoy God's best for your life.

Key No 1: Victory in the Christian life is a gift from God

Paul wrote to the Corinthian church: 'Thanks be to God, who gives us the victory through our Lord Jesus Christ' (1 Cor 15:57). Many Christians fail because they grit their teeth and try to win the victory themselves, instead of receiving it as a gift from God that he is wanting to give them. Remember: God wants you to be victorious every day, and he has done everything necessary to make that possible. You will gain a new insight into the nature of this victorious living as you meditate on the verse 'Now thanks be unto God, which always causeth us to triumph in Christ, and maketh manifest the savour of his knowledge by us in every place' (2 Cor 2:14, AV). The Greek word translated 'triumph' also means 'to have great success', so God wants you and me to be very successful Christians. Unfortunately, success has become a dirty word to many Christians; they somehow think that to be successful is unspiritual and that it is actually spiritual to be unsuccessful! This concept does not come from the word of God! Just think of what God said to Joshua: 'This Book of the Law shall not depart from your mouth, but you shall meditate in it day and night, that you may observe to do according to all that is written in it. For then you will make your way prosperous, and then you will have good success' (Josh 1:8).

Some people will tell you that it is much more important to be faithful than to be successful, but in the parable of the talents Jesus puts these two qualities together (Mt 25:14–30). The servants who were successful in increasing what they had been given for their master were called 'good and faithful' while the unsuccessful servant was told he was 'wicked and lazy'. He thought he was being faithful when he buried the talent he had been given and returned it to his master exactly as he had received it, but Jesus did not share that view. He calls us to be faithful and successful.

Notice, too, that Paul tells us that God 'always causeth us to triumph' (2 Cor 2:14, AV). Most of us change that scripture in our minds to read: 'God sometimes causes us to triumph.' This enables us to settle for an up and down Christian life and convince ourselves that it is the best we can expect. God's plan for us is steady progress upwards in daily triumph which will result in our producing the sweet smell of Christ's presence everywhere we go. The world talks of 'the sweet smell of success', but the real sweet smell of success is the fragrance of the presence of the Lord Jesus Christ who brings us our success. This is the secret of lifestyle witnessing, one of the most effective ways of preaching the gospel that I know.

Key No 2: Faith is the victory

You may have heard the story of the mountaineer who was asked why he wanted to climb a particular mountain and replied, 'Because it is there.' As far as he was concerned, the mountain was only there to be conquered and he was determined to conquer it! Some Christians look at their circumstances which seem like a great mountain blocking their path and ask,

IT'S THE GREATEST DAY YOU EVER LIVED

'How can I possibly have a great day in my circumstances?' Unlike the mountaineer in the story, they seem to think that their mountain is there to conquer them! They need to remember the words of the apostle John: 'This is the victory that has overcome the world —our faith' (1 Jn 5:4). We are called to see the world with all its difficulties and adverse circumstances as something to be overcome by faith. It should not dominate us, we should dominate it. The world has nothing to say to you about what sort of day you are going to have. That depends entirely on your position in Christ as you exercise your faith.

My favourite definition of the world is that it is everything that does not come under the direct lordship of the Lord Jesus Christ. The world would certainly like to overcome us but Jesus says, 'I have overcome the world' (Jn 16:33). As we submit to his lordship, then through our faith in him and in his blood shed for us on the cross, we too can overcome the world. Our faith in Christ's victory on the cross will ensure for us a day of victory today.

Key No 3: Living in the will of God

The kingdom of heaven is the place where Jesus Christ is Lord, and we are living there when our lives are submitted to his will. Jesus himself made this clear when he said, 'Not everyone who says to me, "Lord, Lord," shall enter the kingdom of heaven, but he who does the will of my Father in heaven' (Mt 7:21). Have you a strong desire to do the will of God? Is it the most important thing in your life? Have you a holy fear of being out of God's will? We can gain great confidence from the fact that God loves us and wants us to be in his will, and because of this we can be sure he is not going to make it difficult for us to know his will and do it. It is not hard to know God's will, nor is it any more difficult to do what he wants us to do than to take another course of action. In fact, the Bible tells us that the way of the transgressors is hard. The problem with doing God's will lies in the clash of interests that takes place between God and ourselves. We all have a will of our own and we all like to have our own way, but we begin to live in the kingdom of heaven when we bend our wills to his and say with the Lord Jesus Christ, 'Nevertheless, not as I will, but as you will' (Mt 26:39).

However, before we come to this place we may have a battle royal with him in the area of our wills that might go on for years. God has never lost a battle yet, so when we fight him we are on the losing side and can never live in the victory. On the other hand, when we submit to him and are living in the kingdom of heaven, we are living in his victory and it is impossible *not* to have a great day!

It is a tremendous feeling to lay your head on your pillow at the end of the day and say, 'Thank you, Lord Jesus, for a wonderful day spent in the centre of your will,' and then fall into an untroubled sleep.

Living in God's will is the secret of having great nights as well as great days. Many Christians spend restless nights wondering if they were in the will of God during the past day or whether they will be in his will tomorrow. I have a prayer which reminds me that God is more concerned that I remain obedient to him than I am: 'Lord, before I take one step out of your will, please show me that I am in danger of doing so and lead me back into the place of safety.'

Key No 4: Living and walking in the Spirit

Living in the Spirit is not a passive state; it demands an active walk. As Paul puts it: 'If we live in the Spirit, let us also walk in the Spirit' (Gal 5:25). The secret of this walk is to be found in the previous verse: 'And those who are Christ's have crucified the flesh with its passions and desires' (Gal 5:24).

In practice, this means that we have come to the place where we have died to our own ambitions, desires and plans and have stopped trying to please ourselves. As soon as we begin actively seeking to please him we are walking in the Spirit. We are also producing the fruit of the Spirit, especially self-control, which is another way of saying 'self under his control'.

When the soul dominates the spirit, we yield to temptation and allow ourselves to be enticed away from God's will for our lives (see James 1:14–15). However, when our spirit becomes harnessed to the Holy Spirit, he causes us to walk in step with him, and the character of Jesus is formed in us.

Isaiah says, 'All we like sheep have gone astray; we have turned, every one, to his own way; and the Lord has laid on him the iniquity of us all' (Is 53:6). The alternative to walking in the Spirit is walking in the flesh (Rom 8:1), which is another way of saying 'to have our own way'. When our flesh has been crucified, we will begin to want him to have his way in our lives, and as we begin to follow him, we will soon discover that his way is better than ours every time.

Key No 5: Rejoicing in the Lord all the time

Another key to having a great day is to remember who

made it. As the psalmist said, 'This is the day which the Lord has made; we will rejoice and be glad in it'(Ps 118:24). Today belongs to God and to no one else; he is its Maker and when we have a right attitude towards him we shall also have a right attitude towards everything he has made, including today.

While we hold such an attitude, we are unlikely to have any problems with the day as it passes. All through that day, the only right and proper thing to do is rejoice in God's creation and certainly not to complain and grumble about it. We should enjoy it, and not be miserable in it. The children of Israel, in the wilderness, forgot whose day they were living in and 'murmured against Moses' (Exod 15:24) or as the New International Version puts it, they grumbled. The result was that they spent forty years in the wilderness because they murmured and grumbled about their lot instead of rejoicing and being glad in the day the Lord had given them. To do anything but rejoice in today is to insult its Maker. If you begin each day by praising the Lord for it, you will start off on the right foot and will not have to put things right later on.

The right way to end the day is to be able to say with a glad heart, 'I have sought to do the will of God today and to walk in the Spirit and I feel really fulfilled.' Remember that your life is made up of days and if you are able to rejoice at the end of each one, you will experience the same fulfilment at the end of your life. Then you will be able to say with Paul:

> For I am already being poured out as a drink offering, and the time of my departure is at hand. I have fought the good fight, I have finished the race, I have kept the faith. Finally, there is laid up for me the crown of righteousness,

which the Lord, the righteous Judge, will give to me on that day, and not only to me but also to all who have loved his appearing (2 Tim 4:6–8).

If I reach the end of the day feeling fulfilled, I can sleep soundly, but if not, I fear I have missed something that God has for me. Then a battle begins in my mind and I toss and turn restlessly. Then I recall the scripture, 'There is therefore now no condemnation to those who are in Christ Jesus, who do not walk according to the flesh, but according to the Spirit' (Rom 8:1). I believe that I have been seeking to walk in the Spirit during the day and I confess that according to God's word there is no condemnation for me. Notice that Scripture makes it plain that the time I can enjoy freedom from condemnation is *now*, not when I have prayed a bit more, read my Bible again, or witnessed to a few more people. Neither will that time come only when I get to heaven, it is here now.

The devil is the accuser of the brethren (see Revelation 12:10) and he would love to ruin a great day by bringing you into condemnation at the end of it.

If you are under condemnation, then you will never read your Bible enough or pray enough, and increasing your output in any of these things will never bring you out of condemnation. The only way out is to confess what the word of God says and begin to rejoice and be glad in the day that the Lord has made, declaring that you are not under condemnation. As you do so you can walk free of it.

Key No 6: Resisting the devil

One thing you can be sure of is that if you have had a great day, the devil has had a bad one because of it. You have given him a bad time, but you do not have to let him give you one as well! The Bible says, 'Submit to God. Resist the devil and he will flee from you' (Jas 4:7). How would you like to spend the day running away for someone? Even if you hid yourself away, you would be constantly peeping out to see if your pursuer had caught up with you. Well, that is how the devil should have to live. The only picture I find of the devil in the New Testament, after the crucifixion, is that of a fleeing enemy. Jesus defeated him on the cross and just to remind him of the fact is enough to make him take to his heels. I once heard someone say that when you become a Christian, then God is your Father, Jesus is your elder Brother, the Holy Spirit is your Comforter, and the devil is no relation at all. No wonder he gets out of your way when you realise that!

Key No 7: Trust God's word, not your feelings

If you let them, your feelings will give you plenty of information about your situation, and most of it will be negative. When you get up in the morning and look out of the window, they will tell you that it is raining or snowing or foggy or that the roads are icy or that bad weather is on the way. They will make it clear to you that you can expect to have a bad day and, as time goes by, they will constantly remind you that they were right. When you agree with your feelings, then things are likely to go wrong and give you a bad day. That is a good time to remember that the Bible says, 'Let God be true but every man a liar' (Rom 3:4).

Whatever your feelings or other people may tell you, remember God's word is true. That is the one thing that you can rely on absolutely. Because I believe that God is speaking the truth when he says he makes every day for us to rejoice and be glad in, I can go to bed each night convinced that the following day will be the greatest I have ever known. When I wake up in the morning, I do not have to work myself up into a state of believing that it is going to be a good day; I know it is because God has said so! Yesterday has gone, I am not to worry about tomorrow (Mt 6:34) and I can rejoice in God's now.

I know a man who lives in a very foggy area in Scotland, who gets up on a foggy morning, pulls back his bedroom curtains and says, 'Thank you Lord for a wonderful foggy morning.' When you murmur and complain about the weather, you do not alter it or affect it, but you make sure that it affects you for bad. When you praise the Lord, he affects you for good and you live in his victory.

Key No 8: Making a good confession

To confess God's word is to agree with what he says, so as you make a good confession all day long by saying what God says, you find youself living in the truth of those words. You know that anything you hear from any source which is contrary to the word of God must be untrue, and that you can ignore it. When I find myself in a situation that appears to be impossible, I confess what God says about me: 'I can do all things through Christ who strengthens me' (Phil 4:13). Never say that you cannot do something when God says you can, because his word is always true. The Bible says, 'Let the word of Christ dwell in you richly' (Col 3:16) and I have often noticed that my morning reading was just the word I needed during that particular day to deal with some difficulty or temptation I had to face. If you do not read the word at the beginning of the day and let it dwell in you richly, do not be surprised if things get tough later on.

When Jesus faced the devil in the wilderness, he dealt with his temptations by confessing the word of God to the devil. He said, 'It is written...' (Mt 4:4,7,10) and then quoted an appropriate verse to deal with each of the three temptations he faced. All three verses are to be found in two chapters of Deuteronomy and I believe that Jesus had read them that day as his daily devotions. When the day starts to get you down, confess 'him who is able to keep you from stumbling, and to present you faultless before the presence of his glory with exceeding joy' (Jude 24). Know that God can do that for you today, and expect him to do so.

Key No 9: Keep short accounts with God

Although sin does not now have dominion over us, the possibility of sinning is still with us. This sin can affect our relationship with God, if we do nothing about it, sufficiently to prevent us from having a great day. John reminds us that God has foreseen this problem and made provision for it: 'If anyone sins, we have an advocate with the Father, Jesus Christ the righteous. And he himself is the propitiation for our sins' (1 Jn 2:1–2).

How then can I have a great day when I have sinned? The answer is simple. Do not wait one moment, not

IT'S THE GREATEST DAY YOU EVER LIVED

even until the end of the day, but put things right immediately by confessing your sin to God with a repentant heart. As you do so, 'the blood of Jesus Christ [God's] Son cleanses us from all sin' (1 Jn 1:7). Whatever you are doing, making a cup of tea, scrubbing the floor, driving along the motorway, or wherever you are, go to God immediately and settle the account the Bible way. If you have the gift of tongues then as soon as you have confessed your sin, you can begin to worship God in tongues. You were walking in the flesh when you committed the sin, but as the blood of Jesus cleansed you, then you were lifted right back into the spiritual realm ready to go on walking in the Spirit. Even if you sin, you can still have a great day as long as you keep short accounts with God. He has promised you, 'I, even I, am he who blots out your transgressions for my own sake; and I will not remember your sins' (Is 43:25). If God does not remember your sin, then neither should you. When you have confessed and repented of that sin, you can move into the place of victory knowing you are forgiven and under no condemnation.

You can end that day at peace with God because the blood of Jesus has made it possible. Isn't he wonderful?

You now have nine keys that can open the door to a great day. Keep them in your heart and mind. Believe that the Holy Spirit will bring them to your remembrance when you need them. Use them boldly and step out into a new dimension of living.

2. Don't Settle for Less Than God's Best

As an itinerant evangelist, I stay with all sorts of people, and since we are all different, I am never quite sure what to expect when I visit a home for the first time. However, if it is an English home there is a very strong possibility that before I have been there long, I shall have been invited to have a cup of tea! You know the way the conversation is likely to go!

'Would you like a cup of tea?'
'Yes, please.'
'Milk?'
'Yes, please.'
'How much?'
'Not too much.'
'You'd better say when.'

When it comes to drinking a cup of tea, we all have our own ideas as to how much milk is enough, ranging from none to half a cupful!

When it comes to the Christian life, opinions vary equally widely. If you were to do a survey of the Christians in your locality and ask them some questions on the subject, I suspect that every answer would be different. You might ask:

How much change in your lifestyle is enough?
How much holiness is enough?

How much power of the Spirit is enough?
How much fruit of the Spirit is enough?
How much opening oneself up to other people is enough?
How much prayer is enough?
How much Bible study is enough?
How much of the lordship of Christ is enough?
How many gifts of the Spirit are enough?

Faced with those questions, most of us might be tempted to give the answers that were expected of us, rather than say what we really felt. Jesus asked a blind beggar, Bartimaeus, a similar question when he said to the man, 'What do you want me to do for you?' (Mk 10:51). Putting the story into today's context, Bartimaeus might have made one of several replies:

'I would like a guide dog, please.'
'I would like a white stick, please.'
'Could I have a talking book, please?'
'Could I have some money to buy food, please?'
'If I was just able to see a little, please.'

However, it would appear that his answer to the question, 'How much is enough?' was, 'I want all there is!' His actual reply to Jesus was, 'Rabboni, that I may receive my sight' (Mk 10:51). I sometimes put it like this: 'Fill my cup until it is full and running over, so that others can drink out of the saucer.' Bartimaeus was not willing to settle for less than God's best for him; and neither should we be satisfied with anything less!

Some people are very easily satisfied as we see from the story of the ten lepers recorded in Luke 17:12–19 (AV).

And as he entered into a certain village, there met him ten

men that were lepers, which stood afar off: and they lifted up their voices, and said, Jesus, Master, have mercy on us. And when he saw them, he said unto them, Go shew yourselves unto the priests. And it came to pass, that, as they went, they were cleansed. And one of them, when he saw that he was healed, turned back, and with a loud voice glorified God, and fell down on his face at his feet, giving him thanks: and he was a Samaritan. And Jesus answering said, Were there not ten cleansed? but where are the nine? There are not found that returned to give glory to God, save this stranger. And he said unto him, Arise, go thy way: thy faith hath made thee whole.

Leprosy was a dreadful disease and it had produced a terrible effect on the ten men in the story. Once, they had been ordinary men living normal lives in their village community, but now they were outcasts, separated from families and friends, forced to leave the village and live out in the waste places, in caves or hovels, as best they could, with no one but other lepers in an equally desperate situation for company. They had no money, they were unemployable, and even begging was difficult, because if they ventured into a public place they had to ring a bell and shout, 'Unclean, unclean.' Everyone was afraid of leprosy, so they would keep well away from any lepers. Leprosy is often used as a type of sin in the Bible, for it also splits up families and destroys relationships, damaging communities. It also produces misery and hopelessness, but most of all it separates us from God and keeps us out of his kingdom. Like leprosy, sin forces people to settle for far less than God's best for them.

One grey morning those ten lepers woke up unaware that it was going to be the greatest day they had ever

IT'S THE GREATEST DAY YOU EVER LIVED

lived. Then they heard the news—'Jesus of Nazereth is passing through the village today.' Wasn't he the man who healed the sick? Was it possible that he could do something for them? They made a momentous decision; they would meet him that very day and ask him to help them. One of the ingredients of a great day is to bring Jesus into the now. Some people say, 'I believe Jesus could help me, but I am not sure if it is his time to do so.' The Bible makes it clear that as far as God is concerned, there is only one time to act: 'Behold, now is the accepted time; behold, now is the day of salvation' (2 Cor 6:2, AV).

A friend of mine tells a story about a cup of coffee he never drank on a visit to the USA. He was passing a restaurant one day when he noticed an unusual sign in the window 'Free Coffee Here Tomorrow'. Never being able to resist a bargain, he visited that restaurant again the following day, only to find the sign still in the window, 'Free Coffee Here Tomorrow'. For all he knows, the notice is still there—but no free coffee. The devil would approve of that notice, because his time is always tomorrow. If you listen to him he will tell you that the time to commit your life to Christ, or to be baptised in the Holy Spirit, or to receive your healing is tomorrow. And tomorrow never comes.

Having decided to seize their opportunity and meet Jesus now, the ten lepers were ready when he put in his appearance! They knew if they missed him this time they might never get another chance to do so, and they were desperate men. They wanted to be free from the grip of leprosy and they knew that Jesus was the only One who could set them free.

He is still setting people free today; free from the grip of sin, of sickness, of depression, of poverty and

DON'T SETTLE FOR LESS THAN GOD'S BEST

all the other effects of the curse that God pronounced on Adam after his rebellion in the Garden of Eden. The Bible says, 'For sin shall not have dominion over you' (Rom 6:14) and, 'If the Son makes you free, you shall be free indeed' (Jn 8:36). Freedom is a very common word today, but I often wonder if half the people who use it really know what it means. My definition of freedom is 'to know what is right and have the power to do it'.

There was a young ex-drug addict who gave his testimony in one of my meetings. It was a dramatic story of salvation and deliverance from a powerful drug habit. At one point, the interviewer asked him, 'What does Jesus mean to you?' He thought for a moment before replying and then said simply and with conviction the one word 'freedom'.

Sin and its consequences can dominate our lives in so many ways. It is a driving force that urges us on to do things we do not want to do at all. We can all echo the words of Paul: 'For the good that I will to do, I do not do; but the evil I will not to do, that I practise' (Rom 7:9). He goes on to ask a question and then answer it: 'O wretched man that I am! Who will deliver me from this body of death? I thank God—through Jesus Christ our Lord!' (Rom 7:24–25). It is always a great day when Jesus sets us free from some bondage in our lives, and you can know that freedom now as you follow the example set by the ten lepers.

There are four things about those men that we would do well to note and act on.

IT'S THE GREATEST DAY YOU EVER LIVED

They knew who could help

First of all, they knew who it was who could help them and they cried out, 'Jesus, Master, have mercy on us.' We often sing a chorus in our missions that goes, 'Jesus Is Alive Today.' It is an old chorus now, but the truth it contains is something we need to be constantly reminded of. He is not just an historical figure, a Bible character from two thousand years ago. He is Jesus Christ, 'the same yesterday, today, and for ever' (Heb 13:8). Not only that, we can meet him in as real and effective a way today as those lepers did so long ago! It is that sort of encounter we need to change our lives and set us free from the things that hold us down.

It is not sufficient just to know about Jesus. I know quite a lot about the Queen of England. I know her name and her husband's name. I could give you the addresses of several homes she has. From what I see of her on TV or read in the papers, I often know what she wears, where she goes and what she does. I know a lot about her, but I do not know her. I have never met her or been introduced to her. There has never been a time when I had a personal encounter with her. In the same way, you may know a lot about Jesus that you have read in the Bible, heard about in sermons, or even seen on films or videos about him. But do you know him, have you ever had a personal life changing encounter with him?

When the lepers met him, they called him by his name 'Jesus' and there is something very special about that name. It is called a 'name which is above every name, that at the name of Jesus every knee should bow, of those in heaven, and of those on earth, and of those under the earth, and that every tongue should confess that Jesus Christ is Lord, to the glory of God the Father' (Phil 2:9–11). Peter said, 'There is no other name under heaven given among men by which we must be saved' (Acts 4:12). When we call upon that name as the lepers did, he responds in power to set us free, just as he did for them.

They called him Master

The second thing to note about the ten lepers is that they called him Master. That is equivalent to Prince or Lord. There are many people today who want to know Jesus as Saviour, the one who sets them free from the power of sin, but they may not be willing to have him as Lord of every area of their lives. They say, in effect, 'You can come so far in my life and no further, Jesus.' That means there are areas of their lives over which he does not reign. Some people seeem to get into heaven by the skin of their teeth and spend the rest of their lives sitting on the doorstep of the kingdom of God! Well, it is wonderful to be in the kingdom, even if we are only just inside, but that is certainly not God's full intention for us.

The kingdom of God can be described as the place where Jesus Christ is Lord, and he wants us to live right in that dimension, exploring it and discovering all the treasure it holds for us, because 'God...has blessed us with every spiritual blessing in the heavenly places in Christ' (Eph 1:3). When Abraham moved into Canaan after separating from Lot, God urged him to explore the land that was his inheritance, saying, 'Lift your eyes now and look from the place where you are—northward, southward, eastward, and westward; for all the land which you see I give to you and your descendants for ever...Arise, walk in the land through its length and its width, for I give it to you' (Gen 13:14–15,17). The kingdom is the realm where Jesus is Lord of our lives. If there are areas in which we do not allow him into our lives then there are parts of the kingdom, and spiritual blessings, that are not available to us.

In the parable Jesus told about the great supper (Lk 14:15–24), many of those who were invited did not go, and so never tasted the good things that had been prepared for them. However, just imagine that you had gone to that feast, but after eating the first course you said, 'No thank you, I won't have anything else,' and then sat watching the others enjoying the whole meal. Think what you would have been missing! Let Jesus rule and reign in your whole life, all the time. Let him be Lord of your business, your social life, your relationships, your finance and your spiritual life. He knows how to run your life better than you do, so why not let him?

Because the lepers recognised that Jesus was their Lord, they also realised that he was Lord over their disease. He is Lord of any problem, disease, addiction or habit that may be defeating you. I remember speaking at a meeting in Newcastle with some 1,500 people present. I had been asked to speak on Christ's healing ministry today and then pray for the sick, but with a crowd of that size I did not atempt to pray for each one individually with the laying on of hands. I followed a procedure I have often used in Africa when speaking to large crowds whereby I pray a general prayer for healing and encourage those who are sick to believe that God will heal them as I do so. I often say, 'If you believe that God is going to heal you as I pray, raise an arm.' Then I say, 'The Bible tells us that believers "will lay hands on the sick, and they will recover" (Mk 16:18). You have just said that you believe, so lay your hands on your sick body and God will heal you as I pray.'

Christians who are always talking about themselves, telling everyone what they have done, what they are doing, and what they are going to do, have missed the secret of the Christian life. They do not know what grace is.

My favourite definition of grace is 'something for nothing for those who deserve nothing'. It does not matter how bad we have been, or how good either for that matter, the grace of God is still available to us. Jesus said of the woman who anointed him with the perfumed ointment, 'Her sins, which are many, are forgiven, for she loved much. But to whom little is forgiven, the same loves little' (Lk 7:47). That does not mean that only those who have been great sinners can love God a lot, in order to really love him we have to become aware of the greatness of his grace towards us and of our absolute dependence upon it. Paul describes Christians as 'those who receive abundance of grace' (Rom 5:17). Now abundance means more than enough, and the lepers discovered that although they had done nothing to deserve it, Jesus had sufficient mercy and grace to heal them; all they had to do was ask.

They were united

My fourth point about the lepers is that they knew how to receive from Jesus. When they saw him they 'lifted up their voices'. They were standing afar off from him because of their leprosy, and there would be

IT'S THE GREATEST DAY YOU EVER LIVED

a noisy crowd around Jesus, so unless they made a loud noise they would not be heard. I can just imagine their leader saying, 'Right, you fellows, after three. One, two, three; Jesus Master have mercy on us.' There was real unity among them as they cried out, and that is one of the secrets of receiving great things from God. Our relationships with other Christians need to be right and we need to be in agreement with each other.

Earlier during the meeting, I had seen a crippled man of about twenty-five years of age drag himself into the hall on crutches, helped by his family. I did not realise that he was also blind. He identified himself with my prayer for healing and before I could say 'Amen', he stood up and waved his crutches in the air. Then he paraded up and down in front of the platform where I was standing, shouting, 'I can see, I can see.' No one except Jesus had touched him, but he was completely healed. The last sight I had of him was as he set off to walk home with his mother who was carrying his crutches under her arm. Jesus had shown himself to be the Master of that young man's disease and he is also bigger than any problem you are facing today.

They knew they needed mercy

The third point to notice about the lepers is that they knew what they wanted. They cried out, 'Have mercy on us.' I once heard a preacher say that we are saved by obedience, but I cannot quite agree with that. Obedience is very important, but we are saved by grace (Eph 2:8), and grace and mercy are twins! Whatever your problem, your number one need is for the grace of God in your life.

The realisation of this truth is one of the most important discoveries I ever made in my Christian life. When I was first saved, I did not hear much about the grace of God and I became ensnared in a legalistic mesh of rules and regulations that really had me struggling. Freedom came with the realisation that we are saved by grace through faith, and that salvation is a gift of God. We cannot earn it or win it for ourselves in any way, so that we have nothing to boast about (Eph 2:8–9). How we British people love to boast, but the psalmist got it right when he said, 'My soul shall make its boast in the Lord' (Ps 34:2). We should be boasting in Jesus all the time, wherever we go and whatever we are doing. He should be our constant topic of conversation.

God has joined us together in his body (1 Cor 12:27) and he urges us to endeavour 'to keep the unity of the Spirit in the bond of peace' (Eph 4:3). If we have anything against another Christian, then we need to do something about it, straight away. I have discovered that when someone sets themselves up as my enemy, the best thing I can do is to pray for them that God will bless them more than he blesses me. This is one of the ways of fulfilling his command to love our enemies!

I once heard David du Plessis, who was greatly used by God in the early days of charismatic renewal in the sixties and seventies, speak for one and a half hours on the subject of forgiveness. One of his strong points was the importance of forgiving anyone with whom we are not in complete agreement. That includes people from other churches and denominations whose doctrines differ from ours. I began to put that teaching into practice at once and what a difference it made in my life! Jesus said: 'And whenever you stand praying, if you have anything against anyone, forgive him, that your Father in heaven may also forgive you your trespasses' (Mk 11:25–26). He made that statement when he was talking about getting answers to prayer, and I believe that one of the major hindrances to prayer is having something against someone else as we pray.

You will never have a great day while you are harbouring grudges in your heart. That is a sure way to be a loser and that will be your experience until you put things right and forgive those against whom you have had a grievance.

When you feel hurt by what someone else has done to you, or by what you think they have done, forgive them. That will get rid of your bitterness, envy and resentment against them and set you free to see God move in a mighty way in your life. I am sure that those ten lepers, living together under very difficult and depressing conditions, must have got on each other's nerves sometimes, but they came to Jesus in complete unity. They all wanted to be healed and knew that he was the only one who could help them. Let us allow his love to unite us in him and then let us expect to see answers to our personal and corporate prayers such as we never dreamed before.

One evening during a mission, I spoke on forgiveness and at the end of the meeting a woman came forward for prayer. A colleague counselled her, and was able to bring her to the place where she admitted that she had bitterness in her heart against another member of the family. She asked God's forgiveness and told him that she was going home to make a telephone call that would put things right between herself and the other member concerned. She rose to leave, and then exclaimed in astonishment, 'My arthritis has gone.' She had suffered from a severe arthritic condition for years, but when she confessed her equally long standing resentment, the arthritis went without even being mentioned. My colleague was not even aware she had arthritis until she told him she had been healed!

Jesus told the lepers to go and show themselves to the priests, and as they went they were healed. It was not long before one of them was back again, glorifying God with a loud voice. Jesus asked him, 'Were there not ten cleansed? but where are the nine?' (Lk 17:17, AV). That raises two questions: Where had the nine gone, and: Why had only one returned? I am sure that they had hurried home to be united with their families and friends.

That was a good way of using their new freedom, but *good is often the enemy of the best* and in accepting something good, many people miss God's best for their lives. They settle for less than God's best. Some people are so thrilled at what happened to them when they were saved that they become satisfied where they are and do not go on to seek the baptism in the Holy Spirit. I have heard people say, 'All I want is love, I don't want the gifts of the Spirit as well. I am satisfied with what I have.'

A friend who heard me preaching on this subject wrote a little chorus that we used to sing at our missions in many parts of the world.

> Don't settle for less than God's best,
> Believe for more, believe for more,

> God keeps his promises,
> It is his will to bless,
> So don't settle for less than God's best,
> Believe for more, believe for more.

The man who went back to Jesus to worship and thank him received God's best. The others were cleansed, but he was made whole. I have quoted from the Authorised Version of the Bible at the beginning of this chapter and there two separate words are used; ten were cleansed and one was made whole. The distinction is less clearly seen in some of the more modern translations but two different Greek words were used by Luke and they have different meanings. The first is *katharizo* which means to cleanse, to make clean, to clear. The second is *sozo*, which means to save or make whole.

All ten lepers were cleansed, or made clean, from the active disease of leprosy. They were cleared of the infection, they could no longer spread the disease to others, so the priests would pronounce them to be clean and free to return to the community. However, the disease would have eaten away at their extremities, such as the ends of their fingers, toes, noses and ears, and they would still carry these disfiguring scars. The stumps of their fingers and toes would still be there. I see the one man who was made whole restored to what he had been before the leprosy began to eat away at his body. His fingers, toes, nose and ears would all be restored to wholeness. He would be a walking demonstration of what Jesus meant when he said, 'I have come that they may have life, and that they may have it more abundantly.' Don't settle for less than God's best. Don't be satisfied until you are

DON'T SETTLE FOR LESS THAN GOD'S BEST

living his abundant life.

At one of my very first crusades God performed a miracle that is still fresh in my memory today. A girl of seven brought her four-and-a-half-year-old sister out in the healing line for prayer. I did not have to ask what was the matter with the younger girl; she was cross eyed and it affected her looks badly. As I prayed, God straightened her eyes; everyone could see it happening and they went wild with excitement and began to praise God for what he had done. The little girl went home with her sister without a trace of her condition visible. The following evening, when I invited the sick to come forward for prayer, the little girl came out again and stood with the rest waiting for me to speak to her. I looked at her carefully, but could see no trace of her old condition, so I asked her why she had come forward. She said, 'I have come to thank Jesus for healing me.' I tell you, there was scarcely a dry eye in the meeting at that point. The Bible says, 'A little child shall lead them' (Is 11:6) and this little girl had set us all an example in following the lead of the leper who returned to worship Jesus and receive all God had for him.

I recently had a letter from someone who lives in that town and was present at the meetings where the girl was healed. The writer recalled the miracle and said that the girl has grown up to be a really pretty woman with no trace of her condition.

We so often miss God's best for us and settle for something less because we do not stay close to Jesus, thanking him for all he does for us, and living a life of praise and gratitude to him. He died on the cross in order that we could be made whole, and it is a serious thing to take that provision lightly or be selective in our response to his grace towards us. We must also beware of taking him for granted or using him as a convenience. He died that we might be forgiven and made whole to praise him and glorify him in body, mind and spirit. When we settle for less than his best, we are really spurning him and disappointing him. We glorify him as we demonstrate his abundant life day by day, and each day becomes the greatest day we ever lived.

3. The Book with God in It

Have you ever played the association game, where someone says a word or phrase and you have to reply, without pausing to think, with the word or phrase that springs to your mind in response? I wonder how you would respond to the phrase 'The Bible says'? I guess I would say 'Billy Graham' because anyone who has heard him preach will have heard him use those words frequently. What is more I do not believe those are just empty words on Billy's lips; I am sure that both his life and his ministry are based on what the Bible says because he knows that it is the actual word of God. In this, he is following the best possible example, that of the Lord Jesus Christ himself. Think how he blunted Satan's attack in the wilderness with the words, 'It is written...' (Mt 4:4,7,10).

As we read through the gospel records we discover that the word of God was basic to everything Jesus did; it is abundantly clear that he did not live by bread alone but by every word that proceeded from the mouth of God (Mt 4:4). He lived God's word and that is why he was able to say, 'As I hear, I judge, and my judgment is righteous, because I do not seek my own will but the will of the Father who sent me' (Jn 5:30). He lived by the word of God and eventually died in obeying it, and so set an example for us all.

What importance do you put on God's word in your daily life? Does it determine your lifestyle or is that still moulded by the world's example? The Bible commands us not to be conformed to the world, but to be transformed by the renewing of our mind (Rom 12:2) and we do this by letting the Holy Spirit apply God's word to our mind and mould it to his way of thinking.

Jesus warns us that those who reject him and do not receive his words will be judged by those words in the last day (Jn 12:48). If we do not want to be judged and found guilty by God's word on the last day, we would be wise to judge every situation in the light of that word now, and act accordingly. Circumstances and situations change, but God's word does not change. Jesus said, 'Heaven and earth will pass away, but my word will by no means pass away' (Mt 24:35).

I have sometimes felt under pressure from other Christians who have sought to persuade me to take a certain direction, using strong, powerful, logical arguments to convince me. They succeeded in persuading my mind, but in my heart I still felt ill at ease. In those situations, I have let the word of God be my compass and found that as I have done so, the peace of God has guarded my mind and heart (Phil 4:7). Colossians 3:15 says, 'Let the peace of God rule in your hearts,' and that can be paraphrased, 'Let the peace of God act as an umpire or as an arbitrator in your hearts.' As I base my life on the word of God, I walk in the will of God, and the peace of God assures me that I am still on course. If I do begin to wander, that peace will be disturbed and as I respond to that warning signal, I shall not go far wrong.

THE BOOK WITH GOD IN IT

The Scriptures, which are the word of God, make us wise for salvation (2 Tim 3:15) and we are born again 'through the word of God which lives and abides for ever' (1 Pet 1:23). Once we have been born again, we grow by feeding on that same word as we 'desire the pure milk of the word' (1 Pet 2:2), which will feed us. If we do not read the word, we will not grow. It is as simple as that, and if we do not believe what we read it will do us no good, although it will still judge us in the last day (Jn 12:48).

Failing to believe the word of God is often exemplified in our attitude to the creation story as recorded in the first three chapters of Genesis. As we consider what is stated by many thoelogians, preached in many pulpits and taught in schools concerning those chapters, we can see that they are under a vicious attack, the instigator of which can be no less than the enemy of our souls, the devil. He is well aware that if we doubt the creation story in the Bible, we have begun to develop an unbelieving attitude towards the word of God. If I do not believe the creation story in Genesis, that will affect how I view John 1:3—'All things were made through him, and without him nothing was made that was made,' and, 'By faith we understand that the worlds were framed by the word of God, so that the things which are seen were not made of things which are visible' (Heb 11:3). Having developed this critical, unbelieving attitude towards passages of Scripture related to the creation story, it is easy to apply it to other areas of Scripture without realising what one is doing.

The word of God and victory over sin

John tells us that one of his reasons for writing his first letter had to do with bringing us into victory over sin. 'These things I write to you, so that you may not sin' (1 Jn 2:1). John expected that the words he was writing, which were inspired by God and therefore really God's words, would have the effect of giving us strength against temptation and helping us not to sin. Centuries before John, the psalmist had written, 'Your word I have hidden in my heart, that I might not sin against you' (Ps 119:11). The psalmist was aware that God's word was living in his heart, ready to go to work when it was needed.

Jesus expressed the same idea when he said, 'If you abide in me, and my words in you, you will ask what you desire, and it shall be done for you' (Jn 15:7). Paul put it this way: 'Let the word of Christ dwell in you richly' (Col 3:16). If the word of God is hidden in our hearts, the Holy Spirit will take it out of its hiding place and bring it back to mind when we need it, for example, when we need victory over temptation so that we do not fall into sin (Jn 14:26). However, the Holy Spirit cannot bring to remembrance words that are not in our hearts because we have neglected to read the Bible.

Another way in which the word of God deals with sin is in cleansing after we have sinned or been into a sinful environment. Jesus said, 'You are already clean because of the word which I have spoken to you' (Jn 15:3). Paul speaks of being cleansed by the 'washing of water by the word' (Eph 5:26). This reminds me of the time when Jesus washed the disciples' feet at the last supper (Jn 13:4–11). The disciples had been walking along the hot dusty road and their feet had become stained by the dirt. I guess the disciples would feel dirty and probably smelly too, and after their feet had been washed they would have a nice clean feeling. In just the same way, I often feel dirty and unclean when I have had to spend time in ungodly company, and when I get out of that situation and am able to read the word of God I can feel it cleansing me again. In the same way, I begin to feel dirty if I neglect to read the word of God for a time. When I do turn to it again, I begin to feel all clean inside. It is very similar to the clean feeling you get when having climbed into a bath after getting really grimy, you have a good long soak.

Most of us are aware of areas in our lives where we are particulary weak in resisting temptation, and I have found that studying what the word of God has to say on that subject can be especially profitable. The words I read change me and bring me strength to resist the temptations that come in that area.

I remember counselling a man who came to me for help in an area where he was constantly falling into sin, and I asked him if the fear of the Lord did not check him and hold him back from sin. He said 'no' and added that he really did not know the fear of the Lord, and I told him to go off with his Bible and concordance and find every scripture in the Bible that spoke about the fear of the Lord. I had him divide a sheet of paper into three columns headed respectively: 'Fear of the Lord', 'Little fear of the Lord', 'No fear of the Lord'. I then had him consider carefully each scripture relating to the fear of the Lord in turn and put it under one of the three columns. For example, in Exodus 9:30, Moses said that the reason Pharaoh did not obey the word of God was because he did not fear

IT'S THE GREATEST DAY YOU EVER LIVED

God. My friend had to consider his own attitude when faced with obeying God's word in a situation where he would rather not do so. Was there any fear of God in him at that moment? Did a fear of the Lord affect the way he responded to that scripture? When he reported back to me with his completed list, most of the passages were put in the column 'No fear of the Lord', a few under 'Little fear of the Lord' and none under 'Fear of the Lord'.

I made my friend repeat the exercise every two or three weeks, reading through the scriptures each time and considering what they said before entering them under one column or another. As time passed, the lists changed; soon there were none under the heading 'Little Fear of the Lord', and a few were under 'Fear of the Lord'.

When we ended the exercise, most of the scriptures came under the heading 'Fear of the Lord', with a few under 'Little fear of the Lord', and the 'No fear of the Lord' column was empty. If you feel that you have a weakness in some specific area of your life, turn to the word of God, using a concordance, or getting someone who knows the Bible well to help you in your search, and keep on with that exercise until the word of God has changed you and brought you into the place of victory over sin.

Faith is an essential ingredient of the Christian life, and without faith it is impossible to have a great day. 'The just shall live by faith' (Rom 1:17), 'We walk by faith, not by sight' (2 Cor 5:7), 'Without faith it is impossible to please him' (Heb 11:6). Here again the word of God plays a vital role because 'faith comes by hearing, and hearing by the word of God' (Rom 10:17). However, unbelief can be a hindrance here. If we read the word of God but do not believe it, we are like the Israelites who came out of Egypt with Moses but did not enter the promised land and died in the desert because of unbelief. The Scriptures pass this verdict on them, 'The gospel was preached to us as well as to them; but the word which they heard did not profit them, not being mixed with faith in those who heard it' (Heb 4:2). We know that faith came with the word, but they did not use that faith. Therefore the word did not do them any good and they moved into an area of unbelief. One of the basic causes of this sort of thing is to look on the word of God just as we would look on the words of any man and to read the Bible as if it were just another book.

The man who led me to Christ had a great effect on my life through the things he taught me. Two things he said about the Bible that have stuck with me ever since, and have been a great help to me, were that it was God's personal love letter to me, and that it was the book with God in it. That is why one of the essential ingredients for having a great day is time spent in reading the word of God and meditating on it. The book with God in it makes every day the greatest day you ever lived.

I remember a time when a friend of mine who was in the ministry was going through a dry patch when little was happening. He had become desperate for a deeper reality in his life and one day as he was in prayer, the Lord appeared to him, holding out a Bible, saying, 'All I want is someone who will believe this.' My friend said, 'I will be that man,' and from that moment signs and wonders followed when he preached the word, in a way that had never happened before.

Paul had this to say to Timothy concerning his approach to the word of God: 'Be diligent to present yourself approved to God, a worker who does not need to be ashamed, rightly dividing the word of truth' (2 Tim 2:15). The fact that Paul thought this warning necessary means that we can handle the word wrongly. There are several ways in which we can do this and they all hinder us from having a great day.

1: We can take a text out of its context

Another of those memorable sayings I learnt from the man who led me to the Lord was, 'Take a text out of context and you have a pretext.' Now a pretext is something that conceals the truth rather than revealing it, and by taking it out of its context it is possible to prove almost anything one wants to. I remember Judson Cornwall saying that if he looked in the Bible long enough, he could usually find a verse in one translation or another that he could make support what he wanted to prove. And that is true; if we really want to believe something or to persuade others to believe it, we can usually take a verse of Scripture out of its context and use it to make our point.

I believe that the most heretical sects can be traced back to using a text or texts out of context in this way. If you are not sure what a scripture means, or if you suspect it is being misused in this way, look it up in a concordance and study it in its context, or get a mature Christian friend to help you. Some people find a good commentary useful for guarding against this error.

2: We can be careless in our study of the word of God

Paul called Timothy (and us) to be diligent. I am reminded of the Jews at Berea who 'received the word with all readiness, and searched the Scriptures daily to find out whether these things were so' (Acts 17:11). Of course, we need the inspiration and power of the Holy Spirit to 'rightly divide' the word of truth, but we also need diligence and commitment, to roll up our sleeves and get down to some hard work.

Some Christians have what I would call a super-spiritual attitude towards Bible study. They seem to think that anything systematic by way of Bible study is legalistic. To them, the only valid form of Bible study would be to let the Holy Spirit lead one to open the Scriptures to the right page and read on until one was 'led' to stop. I do believe that the Holy Spirit can work in that way and lead me to open the Bible 'at random', to find when I do so that a certain verse or verses are illuminated and become God's personal word to me at that time. However, I believe that if that is the only method of Bible study we ever use, it becomes very dangerous and can lead to serious errors.

3: We can build a doctrine from one passage of Scripture

It is essential to compare scripture with scripture. Take for example the verse, 'There remains therefore a rest for the people of God' (Heb 4:9). From that one verse, using a little imagination, one could propound a teaching that Christianity is a very passive thing and that God calls us to sit back and do nothing, or at best very little, because he had done it all. If he wants us to have something, he will give it to us. If he wants to heal us, he will do it without us having to ask the elders to pray for us in accordance with James 5:14.

On the other hand, one could start with the verse 'Fight the good fight' (1 Tim 6:12) and build on it a very different teaching. This would depict the Christian life as one long battle, full of strife and earnest endeavour. It would show that the only way to please God is by a life filled with endless activities. The truth, of course, is that in the Christian life there is both rest to enjoy and warfare to be fought, and it is only as we learn from his word what God thinks about these aspects of the Christian life that we can bring our lives into the correct balance.

4: We can judge a promise of God by our own personal experience.

For instance, we could take the verse, 'I am with you always' (Mt 28:20) and say, 'I don't always feel the presence of Jesus with me, so this verse does not mean what it says. It means that he is sometimes with me, sometimes not.' A good rule is that when the word of God and your experience disagree, do not change the word of God, ask him to change your experience. The Bible says, 'Let God be true but every man a liar' (Rom 3:4) and we should never let any human experiences or opinion convince us that God's word is not to be trusted. It is a sound principle that if your experience does not tally with the word of God, you should scrap that experience and get one that does.

I am convinced that God's word, the Bible, says what it means and means what it says, and that God will do what he has said he will do. When we read

God's word, we are dealing with God himself and therefore we must not dismiss that word as irrelevant or treat it lightly as if it were fallible like the words of men.

Slaves do not enjoy great days, but if a slave was suddenly set free from his shackles, I guess he would go out and have a great day enjoying his new-given freedom. Jesus said, 'If you abide in my word, you are my disciples indeed. And you shall know the truth, and the truth shall make you free' (Jn 8:31–32). A disciple of Jesus is someone who makes Jesus' word his home, as the Jerusalem Bible puts verse 31. God's word is truth (Jn 17:17) and that truth sets us free (Jn 8:32). As we gladly receive God's word (Acts 2:41) we are set free to be glad and to have a great day.

Finally, we see that because Jesus was the Word made flesh (Jn 1:14), as we spend time in God's word, we are spending time with Jesus and getting to know him better. The closer we are to Jesus, the better the day. Remember, the truth sets us free, and Jesus is the truth (Jn 14:6). The Greek word translated truth can also mean reality, so as we let the word of God dwell in us richly, reality comes into our lives and we begin to live in the real world, not the cloud-cuckoo-land where so many spend their lives. You cannot have a great day in cloud-cuckoo-land, because there can never be any reality there.

James tells us that if we only listen to God's word but do nothing about it, we are deceiving ourselves. We are like the man in Jesus' parable who built his house on the rock (Mt 7:24–27). He thought that his life was secure and that he was going to have a great day, but in fact his life collapsed around him when the storm broke. The man who was a doer of the word built on a foundation of solid rock and had a great day. Notice that the two men heard the same word, in the same way, at the same time. They could have been two men sitting next to each other at a meeting. The difference between the two men and what happened to them lay in what they did with the word they heard. One took action on the word he heard, the other took none. The result was that the same day was for one a disastrous day and for the other a great day.

I invite you to join the man who built on the rock and had a great day when the storm was raging all around him.

Read the word of God.
  Hear God speaking in it.
    Do what it says.
      Let it become life in you.
        Live in reality.
          Have a great day.

4. Hearing from Heaven

We all like to hear some good news, something to encourage us and cause us to look forward to the future with more confidence. However, before we get too excited about what we hear, we need to consider where it comes from, because its source will determine its value. Words are meaningless when the speaker has no power to put them into effect, or is unreliable and cannot be trusted. God is the only One who never makes a promise he is unable to fulfil and whose word is totally reliable. It is for that reason that I often say that I would rather hear from heaven than from Buckingham Palace, 10 Downing Street, or the White House. All I would hear from any of those places would be the voice of man, but when I hear from heaven, I hear the voice of God.

Sounds from heaven

The Bible is full of stories of men who heard a sound from heaven that changed their world. One such man was Gideon (Judges 6–8). When he was a young man, God's people were in disarray and under the heel of the oppressor because they had rebelled against God and gone after other gods. As is always the case, these

IT'S THE GREATEST DAY YOU EVER LIVED

practices led to fear and the Israelites were terrified of the Midianite invaders. When Gideon heard from heaven he was threshing corn in a winepress to keep it from the Midianites. It had not been a good day up to that point and it is doubtful if Gideon even knew what a good day was! His knowledge of God was limited to stories of what he had done for his people in a bygone age. There was no present reality of God in Gideon's life.

When Gideon responded positively to the voice from heaven, God came back on the scene and before long there had been a dramatic change for the better in the condition of God's people. They had been set free from the Midianites, were worshipping the living God, and were enjoying his blessing. They, along with Gideon, were learning what a great day was really like. Gideon was also learning to hear the voice from heaven more promptly, and that led to the rout of the Midianites in battle. Among the many other Bible characters who heard from heaven we could mention Moses, Joshua, Elijah, Isaiah and Paul who all, as a result, made a lasting impact on the world.

However, the greatest example of someone who heard from heaven and changed the world was Jesus himself. He said:

> I am able to do nothing from Myself—independently, of My own accord; but as I am taught by God and as I get His orders. [I decide as I am bidden to decide. As the voice comes to Me, so I give a decision.] Even as I hear, I judge and My judgment is right [just, righteous], because I do not seek or consult My own will—I have no desire to do what is pleasing to Myself, My own aim, My own purpose—but only the will and pleasure of the Father Who sent Me (Jn 5:30, AMP).

HEARING FROM HEAVEN

I am sure that the days Jesus spent with his disciples were great days, because he always obeyed his Father. The secret of a great day is to hear from heaven and do what God tells you to do.

The men and women down the years in Christian history who did great things for God are those who heard from heaven.

At a conference some years ago, God spoke to me and showed me that he wanted instant not eventual obedience. I guess that many of us are a bit like Jonah who is a typical example of eventual obedience. Like him, we may have initially tried to escape the voice from heaven and make our own decisions, pleasing ourselves not God, only to find, as Jonah did, that this led to turmoil which only ceased when we eventually did obey God. For Jonah, the fish's belly must have been a very unpleasant place and like him many of us have found ourselves in very unpleasant circumstances which could have been avoided if we had only obeyed the voice of God in the first place.

Joshua is an excellent example of instant obedience. The instructions that God gave him for the conquest of the fortress of Jericho were unusual, but he just went right on and carried them out. As he obeyed the voice from heaven, he found those instructions worked. Noah is another man who heard some strange words from heaven when God told him to build an ark. Just imagine how it must have felt to build that boat in a desert, far from the ocean, under a cloudless sky while the locals mocked and derided him. These examples teach us that if we are going to obey the voice from heaven instantly we have to learn to cope with the unusual. The walls of Jericho crumbled because when God spoke, Joshua and his men obeyed.

IT'S THE GREATEST DAY YOU EVER LIVED

A married couple came to me for help on one occasion and told me how they had struggled to live the Christian life for many years. Their marriage was a disaster; they had both committed adultery and constantly fought each other, sometimes literally. All this brought inevitable damage to their children.

Outwardly their Christian life looked reasonable enough; they attended church regularly and had gone forward to be counselled at the crusades conducted by very well-known and respected evangelists. Yet under the surface, their lives were in a mess. Having attended this meeting at which I was the speaker, they had responded and come forward to be counselled, but it was obvious that the counsellor who had spoken to them had not been able to help. I began by asking them a question, 'What did God say to you tonight that caused you to come forward?' The husband replied, 'It was something that I have never heard before, that you need to give your whole life to God, and not just ask him for forgiveness.' While it was true that he had never heard it said, that did not mean that it had never been spoken in his presence. I very much doubt that I was the first to speak of giving your whole life over to God. It may well be that as it was said before, he hardened his heart to it, and so did not hear.

I believe that this is why many Christians struggle throughout their lives, going round in circles and getting nowhere. The children of Israel, who, as we have already noted, spent forty years in the wilderness doing this because they had hardened their hearts (Heb 3:15), could have done the whole journey from the Red Sea to the river Jordan in eleven days. They had come out of Egypt, but hardened their hearts against obeying God and going into the promised land because of the difficulties they saw ahead of them.

Eight people were saved when a flood destroyed the rest of mankind because Noah heard from heaven and built the ark exactly according to God's design. In the same way, the heroes of faith of whom we read in Hebrews 11 did great exploits because they heard and obeyed his voice.

The Bible tells us, 'Faith cometh by hearing, and hearing by the word of God' (Rom 10:17, AV). All the men we have been considering heard from God, and then acted in faith, with the result that they did great exploits. They also give us clear directions on how to hear and act in faith

While counselling, I have often heard people say, 'God never speaks to me.' One very common reason why we do not hear God speak is because we have rebelled against something he has already said to us and instead of obeying him we have hardened our hearts to his word. The Bible says, 'Today, if you will hear his voice, do not harden your hearts as in the rebellion' (Heb 3:15). While we complain that God never speaks to us, he is patiently waiting for us to listen to what he is already saying! When we do repent of our hardness of heart and begin to hear him again, we find that he is still repeating what he was saying when we decided that we did not want to hear him! God has, however, promised us that when we repent and cry out to him for help, then, 'Your ears shall hear a word behind you, saying, "This is the way, walk in it"' (Is 30:21).

Here is the link between hearing from heaven and walking in a close relationship with God, and it brings us the challenge: How deep is our experience with him in reality?

In the same way, many evangelicals have come to the Lord for forgiveness but harden their hearts against coming right into the kingdom of God, under the rule and reign of Christ in every area of their lives. They prefer to retain some control over their life. However, Jesus warns us, 'Whoever desires to save his life will lose it, and whoever loses his life for my sake will find it' (Mt 16:25). As Christians, we are saved to live in the kingdom of God. 'Unless one is born again, he cannot see the kingdom of God' (Jn 3:3) and, 'Unless you are converted and become as little children, you will by no means enter the kingdom of heaven' (Mt 18:3). You cannot live in reality in the kingdom of God unless you know the King and submit to his lordship in every area of your life. That is why many Christians, having come to the cross for forgiveness, spend many years wandering in a wilderness situation. The kingdom of God is a theocracy, and a super definition of a theocracy I once heard is 'a place where you do not get a vote on what the King says'.

That night, when I finished talking to the Christian couple, they gave their whole lives to God and today they are part of the ministry team of their local church. There has also been a real improvement in their marriage.

When Peter was defending himself before the Sanhedrin, he said, 'We are his witnesses to these things, and so also is the Holy Sprit whom God has given to those who obey him' (Acts 5:32). One of the old choruses I would sing enthusiastically in the early days of my Christian life was 'Where he leads me I will follow'. We will never be led by the Holy Spirit until we come to the place where we are willing to follow. This is essential to our developing relationship with God as we come to the place where we hear and obey his voice daily.

The first miracle recorded in John's gospel, that of turning the water into wine at the marriage at Cana in Galilee, must have been a real test to the servants who had filled the water pots at Jesus' command. They then had to pour out some of that water and take it to the Governor of the feast and the guests who were calling for the wine. To the natural man the whole thing would seem utterly ridiculous, but Mary had said, 'Whatever he says to you, do it' (Jn 2:5). They obeyed his command to draw some of the water and take it to the Governor of the feast, in faith that he knew what he was doing and that if they obeyed him, all would be well. We can never divorce faith and obedience.

In chapter 6 we will see that Peter's response of faith and obedience to his Lord's command 'Come' was to get out of the boat. If he had not done that, he would never have walked on the water. I recently reduced my weight by some 50lbs. This was quite noticeable and many people came up to me and asked me how I did it. I usually teased them by telling them that my secret would cost them £100. My reason for saying this was that most people just would not have believed what the secret was if I had told them bluntly, so I played them along a little to emphasise my point. Right down at the bottom line, the truth was simply that I heard God speak to me and tell me to get my weight down.

I had struggled for several years with various diets, and several people, including my wife and doctor, had told me that I really should lose some weight, but nothing was ever permanently successful. I would always lose a little weight and then put it all back on again. The real key to the change and my eventual success was that because I had heard God speak to me I did not have an option. The result of this was that I lost 50lbs in weight. The Christian life would be so much easier for us if we all came to the place where we were so sold out to God that when he spoke we did not consider that we had an option, but just obeyed him, instantly without question.

Our unbelief is the greatest hindrance to us reaching this position. God can only speak to faith and if we are in unbelief when we hear that, we usually begin to analyse what we hear by saying, 'Is it me? Is it God? Is it the devil?' Another hindrance is the very casual in-and-out life we have with God. As a result, we sometimes do not recognise when it is God speaking to us. One effect of unbelief is to harden our Christian life and service into set patterns. Simon Peter had a struggle on this point when God spoke to him from heaven, telling him to go and preach the gospel to Cornelius, the Roman centurion, and his household. He had heard Jesus say to the Canaanite woman, 'I was not sent except to the lost sheep of the house of Israel' (Mt 15:24). Now here was Jesus telling him to do just the opposite. This spoilt the neat little rule Peter had got into his head on the subject, and in addition he probably found the prospect of going to Cornelius disturbing for several reasons. What kind of reception would he get there? More important, perhaps, what would his Jewish Christian colleagues have to say about it?

So Peter's first reaction to God's voice from heaven

was, 'Surely not, Lord,' (Acts 10:14, NIV). Fortunately for Peter, he was eventually willing to obey God's voice.

Like Peter, we need to be willing to break out of the set patterns that rule our Christian lives. I often hear, in counselling situations, how the person seeking help has been baptised in the Holy Spirit and spoken in tongues, but feels that he has no power in his life. The issue here is in discerning the power of the Holy Spirit. Power is not a feeling. It can certainly be expressed within us by a confidence in God, but we can only truly discover what it is when we take action and obey his voice. I once heard a very good friend of mine, Cecil Cousen, talk about an occasion when he attended a meeting conducted by another minister, where the power of God was being displayed in a remarkable way. Cecil thought to himself, 'I have often preached these things, but never seen them happen in my meetings. When this man preaches them, they happen.' From then on, he began to look to God to do the things that he was speaking about in his own meetings.

I was told when I began my own ministry that I should always expect God to do what I preached, right there in the meeting. We need to ask ourselves the question: Is the reason for an absence of power in my Christian life unbelief which makes me unwilling to take steps of faith and do the unusual things that God is telling me to do? That word 'unusual' can include new things that are outside of my present realm of experience. They may be the things that are commonplace to some other Christians, but something that I have not done before.

When Jesus was about to make his truimphal entry

IT'S THE GREATEST DAY YOU EVER LIVED

into Jerusalem, he needed a colt to ride on. He told his disciples where they would find the animal, one that had never been ridden before. The disciples were to untie it and bring it to Jesus and he told them what to say if anyone asked them what they were doing (Mt 21:1-3). To the disciples these must have been very strange instructions, but they obeyed them. This was an expression of their commitment to the Lord and their willingness to obey him when it meant launching out into the unknown beyond anything they had previously experienced.

Paul described himself as a prisoner of the Lord (Eph 3:1). We too, need to become love slaves of the Lord Jesus Christ. There is a whole new realm of relationship with him here that is not only exciting and thrilling, but also deeply challenging. I believe God is inviting us to move into that place and live there. Are we willing to accept the challenge to volunteer to become his love slaves? In doing so, we have to abandon the right to quit. It is true that quitters never win and winners never quit. We become winners as we become more sensitive to his voice and learn to hear from heaven every day. Then every day will be a great day.

On my way to London airport, as I was about to set off on one of my visits to Chile, I attended a meeting at a London church. Someone prophesied over me saying, 'God has chosen a rich farmer to take care of you.' I had no idea that there were any problems with the Chile itinerary, but when we arrived at Santiago we were told that they were having problems with finding us accommodation at Osorno, a two hour flight south from Santiago. We were spending the first night in Santiago in an evangelist's home and before we had been there an hour we had a phone call from Osorno to say that God had answered their prayers concerning our accommodation. A rich farmer had made his luxury town apartment available to us for the duration of the crusade there.

Can you imagine what it did for us? God had spoken to us and given us his answer to our need before we were even aware of it. That certainly produced in me a new confidence in God and had a significant effect on the Osorno crusade.

It is my prayer that God will speak to you today, and that you will respond with instant obedience, as you enjoy the greatest day you ever lived.

5. It Moved

Have you ever been lost? It can be a frightening feeling to realise that you are in unfamiliar surroundings, that you do not know where you are. Everything looks strange and people seem unfriendly. You feel disorientated and bewildered and this could easily lead to panic. What a relief it is to spot some familiar landmark or see a face you recognise. You begin to feel safe again. You have an inner feeling of, 'There's a welcome sight' or, 'Am I pleased to see you!' Familiar places and old friends make us feel safe and secure, while the unfamiliar tends to produce fear and insecurity. For most of us, changes in our routines, a move to a new environment, meeting new people, all tend to produce feelings of fear and insecurity. We feel this is different and we don't like it. A common reaction is to try and restore things to normal as quickly as possible before they get out of hand and take control over us.

When I was in Romania I heard a Baptist pastor tell an apparently true story about a man who went for a walk in the countryside with his little daughter. As they strolled along, they came across a very beautiful insect, motionless on the ground in front of them. The father stopped his daughter, motioned to her to stay very still and quiet, and then drew her attention to the insect. She was completely enraptured by its beauty and stood staring in fascination for a long time. Then her father began to talk to her about it quietly and she told him that she thought that it was the most remarkable and attractive insect she had ever seen. It really was a lovely creature. Then suddenly the girl stopped talking and brought her foot down hard on the insect, killing it instantly. Her father was startled and when he recovered from his surprise he asked her why she had done it. Without hesitation, she replied, 'It moved.'

During the past few years, the Holy Spirit has been moving in a very powerful way wherever God's people have given him the freedom to do so and have responded to his promptings. I have, however, been involved in a number of different churches where, although this freedom was granted at first, it was later withdrawn and his work came to a full stop. God told Job that he had fixed boundaries for the ocean saying, 'This far you may come, but no farther, and here your proud waves must stop!' (Job 38:11). God has the right and authority to say this to any part of his creation, but it is not wise for man to say it to his Creator! It is an awesome thing to limit God's movement in our lives and churches.

The Bible's verdict on the generation of Israelites who came out of Egypt with Moses, is that they 'limited the Holy One of Israel' (Ps 78:41). They came out of Egypt and passed through the Red Sea, and even crossed the desert reasonably quickly, until they came to the Wilderness of Paran (Num 12:16) when Moses sent out the spies into the Promised Land. Then, in spite of the evidence they had of God's ability

IT MOVED

to keep them and fulfil his plans for them, they limited that ability in their hearts and refused to move on when he called them to do so. The Bible describes this limiting of God as disobedience and unbelief (Heb 3:18–19).

How different was the attitude of Billy Bray, the great Cornish contemporary of John Wesley, who said that God is not limited, and added that he belonged to the company called 'Father, Son and Holy Ghost Unlimited'. Because of this attitude, God was able to use him in a time of revival in Cornwall.

He went out with no visible finances or resources of any kind and built a number of churches in the most unlikely spots. God paid all the expenses and filled every one of the churches to overflowing. Billy Bray gave God room to move in Cornwall and as a result God extended his kingdom and church there in an awe-inspiring way.

It is a sobering fact that we are the only part of God's creation to which he gave the ability to say 'no' to him. He gave us the power to limit his power in our lives and in our churches! He did establish his kingdom in the Promised Land of Canaan but not with that original generation that Moses led out of Egypt. They spent forty years in the wilderness going round in circles, although as we have seen the actual distance from the Red Sea to the Promised Land was only an eleven-day journey. It has been said that it was a lot easier for God to get the children of Israel out of Egypt than it was for him to get Egypt out of the children of Israel.

God made us with the ability to form habits, and that can be a very useful attribute. For instance, the habits I formed as a boy prevented me spending hours each morning wondering which sock to put on first when I got out of bed or whether I should put on my trousers before my shirt, or vice versa. By getting dressed in my habitual way I complete the whole operation in a few minutes.

My colleague Mike Darwood told me of an interesting experience he had on a training course for craft instructors. The students were paired off and one had to write on a piece of paper all the things he did when he got into his car in the morning to the point where the car started moving. Mike completed his list and then had to go out to his car and start it to see if he had missed anything.

He found that he had to add several operations and then he went through the procedure again while his partner checked his list to see if he had still forgotten anything. The partner noticed that Mike did several things, such as adjust his driving mirror and seat position, that were not written on the list, since he did these things by habit and was not even conscious that he was doing them. I guess it would not have been easy to teach him to change his procedure for driving off in his car in the morning.

In the same way we have formed traditions and established habits in our Christian lives both as individuals and as part of the church to which we belong. After a time, some of these things become very firmly rooted in our lives and we may not even be conscious that we do them! They can be a tremendous hinderance to God when he wants to bring change into our lives and churches. From my experience of being involved in a number of churches that have begun to move forward with God and then ground to a halt, it seems to me that the more powerfully he moves in a situation, the greater the barriers of habit

IT MOVED

and tradition that we erect to prevent him from achieving his purpose. Our memories of past blessings discourage us from departing from our old established ways, and allowing the Holy Spirit to move us on into something new and better. The truth is that God will never take us back into bondage or less productive ways; his way is always forward into greater blessings —even if the road to them is sometimes steep and stony.

We need to break out of the bondages of traditions, customs and old habits, in the power of the Holy Spirit.

Paul exhorts us: 'Stand fast therefore in the liberty by which Christ has made us free, and do not be entangled again with a yoke of bondage' (Gal 5:1). He also says:

> Not that I have already attained, or am already perfected; but I press on, that I may lay hold of that for which Christ Jesus has also laid hold of me. Brethren, I do not count myself to have apprehended; but one thing I do, *forgetting those things which are behind* and reaching forward to those things which are ahead, I press towards the goal for the prize of the upward call of God in Christ Jesus (Phil 3:12–14, italics mine).

'Stand fast', in the sense that Paul uses it, includes moving on into all the new things that God has in store for us. As we enjoy our freedom to keep what we have and move forward into his plans for our future, we shall be constantly enjoying the greatest day we have ever lived. On the other hand, it is not possible to have a great day when we are bound by our past experience.

Paul's statement that he forgot what was behind

him, is often applied by preachers to bad and negative things in our lives, and we certainly do need to be set free from them. However, from the context of the verse, it seems that Paul may also have had good things in mind and these can also hold us back. God wants us to have the very best and that often necessitates leaving the good things we have behind and letting the Holy Spirit take us where we have never been before. When the Israelites were finally poised to cross Jordan into the Promised Land, Joshua told them to keep close to the priests bearing the Ark of the Covenant, 'That you may know the way by which you must go, for you have not passed this way before' (Josh 3:4). They obeyed Joshua and moved safely into their inheritance.

Remember the words of the angel Gabriel to Mary when he told her that she was to be the mother of Jesus: 'For with God nothing will be impossible' (Lk 1:37). And of the Lord Jesus Christ: 'He who believes in me, the works that I do he will do also; and greater works than these he will do' (Jn 14:12). I believe that many Christians find these words a great embarrassment and I have heard some ingenious attempts by preachers to explain them away or to show that they only apply to the preaching of the gospel and not the miracles. However, we ignore them at our peril, and I for one am convinced that Jesus knew exactly what he was saying, and meant it. His words will come to pass; are you prepared to let them happen in your life and your church? Or are you saying to him in effect, 'I will only allow you to come so far and no further; these things are not going to happen as far as I am concerned?'

Complacency can be a real stumbling block both to

the individual Christian and to the church. We feel that we have made a lot of progress and that it would be nice to settle down for a time and leave the pioneering to others, at least for a season. We feel that we deserve a rest. However, this is a very risky position to get into, and it is quite likely that before long we would fall asleep spiritually and become impotent in the kingdom of God. We would stop moving on with God and would lose the pioneering spirit that is essential if we are to continue to develop into maturity. This is particularly important for anyone who has any sort of leadership role in their church. A complacent leader is like a cork in a bottle or, to change the metaphor, he is particularly prone to putting his foot down hard on any move of God and killing it in his church before it has got properly started.

We need to have a pioneering spirit. In this, we can have no better example than Abraham who 'obeyed when he was called to go out to the place which he would afterwards receive as an inheritance. And he went out, not knowing where he was going' (Heb 11:8). There was a man who 'boldly went where no man has gone before'!

One of the areas into which the Holy Spirit desires to lead us today is into a fulfilment of Christ's promises: 'Most assuredly, I say to you, he who believes in me, the works that I do he will do also; and greater works than these he will do, because I go to my Father' (Jn 14:12). I believe that this will take us beyond the things that we read of in the Acts of the Apostles into all the miraculous works Jesus performed himself when he was on earth.

I challenge you to dare to believe, with me, that in

IT'S THE GREATEST DAY YOU EVER LIVED

this generation ordinary Christians like us will walk on water, feed thousands with a few bread rolls and some pilchards, change water into wine, raise the dead, pay the rates with a coin from the fish's mouth. From reports I hear it would seem that most of these things have already happened somewhere in the world during the last few years. In particular, Arthur Wallis in his book *China Miracle* has some amazing stories, including miracles of healing and angelic visitations.

You may find it hard to believe that such events are occurring today, even in far away China, and it may be even more difficult for you to see them happening in your town, with you involved. I personally do believe that every miracle recorded in the New Testament will have its parallel among those Christians who are to step out in faith before Jesus returns.

All leaders have an awesome responsibility for making sure that God has room to move in their church. I remember being told at the beginning of my ministry, 'Let the Holy Spirit loose in your meeting and anything can happen.' I have found this to be an invaluable piece of advice over the past twenty-five years as I have sought to give the Holy Spirit his rightful place in my meetings, with freedom to move as he chooses. You must have heard of Mr Heinz whose company became famous for selling '57 Varieties'. The Holy Spirit can easily beat that record —in fact he could be called the Spirit of infinite variety. I do not believe that any two of our meetings should ever be alike. The most effective programme for any meeting is a sensitivity to the leading of the Holy Spirit.

One of the most important points we need to grasp is that just because something is different does not mean that it is wrong, nor, if it is right, does it mean that the thing it replaces was wrong! We can be right, change and still be right! Many of us have difficulty in coping with change, and this can be a hindrance to a new move of the Holy Spirit. We need to develop an adventurous, pioneering attitude that will enable us to move into new areas of experience as the Holy Spirit leads us. Then we will be able to lead others into that same experience and we will no longer be corks in bottles, but shoehorns to ease feet into new shoes!

Some might hesitate when faced with a new area of ministry, out of a fear that it might not be the work of the Holy Spirit but that of Satan. My reaction in such a situation is to check to see if it is in the Bible. If it is, I want it, otherwise I want nothing to do with it.

We have already noted the Bible's warning, 'Where there is no vision, the people perish' (Prov 29:18, AV). It is also true that where there is a very restricted vision, the church stagnates. I am sure that God is longing for us to expand our vision even though for many of us there has been a great expansion already during recent years. In many churches I know, God has much more room to move today than he had twenty-five years ago when I began my ministry, but in spite of that he wants us to go a lot further yet. There are still millions of people whom the church has not yet reached, so there is plenty of room for increased efficiency. We should have such a burning desire to reach those lost millions that we will allow nothing to stand in our way in our efforts to do so.

Although all these truths are of vital importance to leaders, they are also essential for every Christian. I am convinced that evangelism is at its most effective when it is body ministry with the whole church involved. The whole body will then move forward in the power of the Holy Spirit, giving God room to move and work among us.

The Lord Jesus Christ is coming back for a church 'not having spot or wrinkle or any such thing' (Eph 5:27). We must be careful not to hinder that work by limiting God's movement among us. We must remember the lesson of the little girl who was at one moment moved by the beauty of the insect she saw and the next terrified by it when it began to move. She was so overcome by her fear that she put her foot down hard on it and killed it. No doubt her fear was due, at least in part, to her uncertainty as to what it would do if she allowed it to continue to move, and I believe that many people say no to God and will not allow him freedom to move in their lives and churches because they are apprehensive as to what might happen if they did.

It is equally disastrous to say, 'Well, that's great for others in their churches, it looks really beautiful there, but it's not for us.' This attitude is again the result of fear of the unknown. This is a destructive and restricting fear, but God's 'perfect love casts out fear' (1 Jn 4:18).

Let us put our trust in God's unquestionable love and push back the boundaries of our faith, expecting him to lead us into new realms of revelation in our day. Then the Holy Spirit will be free to work among us and bring us into all God has for us.

6. How to Walk on Water

> Where lies the land to which the ship would go?
> Far, far ahead, is all her seamen know,
> And where the land she travels from? Away
> Far, far behind, is all that they can say.

The poet A H Clough who penned the above lines is but one of many literary figures who have been fascinated by the concept of life as a voyage. He goes on to speak of 'sunny noons' when life on that voyage is really pleasant, but he also mentions 'stormy nights when wild north-westers rave', and as we are all aware from painful experience, we encounter plenty of storms in life's voyage.

There are times when everything seems to be going wrong and although we struggle and toil with all our might we feel that we are making no progress. The gospels of Matthew, Mark and John all include accounts of a storm the disciples experienced when they set out to cross the Sea of Galilee after the feeding of the five thousand, leaving Jesus alone praying in the hills. At first, they seem to have made progress, but soon they were 'straining at rowing, for the wind was against them' (Mk 6:48). 'The boat was now in the middle of the sea, tossed by the waves, for the wind

IT'S THE GREATEST DAY YOU EVER LIVED

was contrary' (Mt 14:24).

The disciples found that there was a way through the storm to their goal and so can we, with Christ's help. In both this and the following chapter, we shall be considering how to deal with the storms of life, using the disciples' experience in the storm on the Sea of Galilee as the basis of our study. The Bible is also full of other examples of the storms of life, one being the whole journey of the Israelites from Egypt to the Promised Land. They started off in high hopes after Pharaoh let them go, but it was not long before a succession of storms began to slow them down. The first of these arose when they found themselves trapped between the Red Sea and Pharaoh's army, and later on there were times when they were in danger of dying of thirst, or starvation, or snake bites or being overcome by other problems. On every occasion, God intervened and took them through the storm, but when the next one blew they forgot his past help and began to founder. In fact, only two of that generation did reach their goal; the rest where drowned in a sea of unbelief.

Probably the most common ways of reacting to the storms of life are either to give up or to grit one's teeth and struggle on, determined to make the best of a bad job, resigned to the fact that life is going to be one long struggle with little or nothing to show at the end of it. If you put yourself in one of these categories, I have some good news for you! You do not have to give up, and God does not want you to make the best of a bad job, nor to fight a constant battle against overwhelming odds without getting anywhere in the normal Christian life. At the end of his life, which included more that its fair share of storms, Paul could say, 'I have fought the good fight, I have finished the race, I have kept the faith. Finally, there is laid up for me the crown of righteousness, which the Lord, the righteous Judge, will give to me on that day, and not only to me but also to all who have loved his appearing' (2 Tim 4:7–8). You can be among the others who share Paul's triumphant experience.

There is no evidence that Adam toiled in the Garden of Eden before he sinned; in fact Genesis 3:17–19 makes it clear that toil is connected with the curse God pronounced on mankind as a consequence of sin.

> Then to Adam [God] said, 'Because you have heeded the voice of your wife, and have eaten from the tree of which I commmanded you, saying, 'You shall not eat from it': 'Cursed is the ground for your sake; In toil you shall eat from it all the days of your life. Both thorns and thistles it shall bring forth for you, and you shall eat the herb of the field. In the sweat of your face you shall eat bread till you return to the ground, for out of it you were taken; for dust you are, and to dust you shall return.'

Jesus died to set us free from the effects of that curse, so Christians do not need to face a life of fruitless toil. When Jesus saw his disciples 'toiling in rowing' (Mk 6:48, AV) he immediately took steps to change that situation. He also said on another occasion, 'Come to me, all you who labour and are heavy laden' (Mt 11:28), which is surely a description of toiling, and went on to offer his hearers rest. I believe he was speaking particularly to people who were toiling and striving to please God by observing all the religious duties laid down by the Law and the scribes. There are many today who are also toiling to overcome the storms of life by increased religious activity. They feel unworthy, guilty and conscious of sin and the fact that they deserve nothing from God. However, instead of relying on his grace and mercy, they strive to win his approval by many and varied means which could include prayer, Bible study, fasting, attending meetings, witnessing and taking communion. We should all be involved in these things, but as an expression of the life of Christ within us, not in order to win his approval.

It is interesting to study Matthew's account of the storm on the Sea of Galilee (Mt 14:22–33), paying particular attention to the way Peter reacted to it. I love to study the life of Peter; he is a tremendous character who has a great deal to teach us about living the Christian life. In this incident, he teaches us that storms are made to walk on! They are not there to fill us with fear and unbelief, to cause us to make shipwreck or to drown us. To the natural eye, walking on the water must be just about the most unlikely way of overcoming a storm at sea, but when it is done by faith in God and in the power of the Holy Spirit, it proves to be the best way. The Christian should always 'walk by faith, not by sight' (2 Cor 5:7). If you try walking on the water by sight you will sink because you will be attempting the impossible.

Matthew tells us how Peter changed from walking by faith to walking by sight:

> [Jesus] said, 'Come.' And when Peter had come down out of the boat, he walked on the water to go to Jesus. But when he saw that the wind was boisterous, he was afraid; and beginning to sink he cried out, saying, 'Lord, save me!' And immediately Jesus stretched out his hand and caught him, and said to him, 'O you of little faith, why

did you doubt?' And when they got into the boat, the wind ceased (Mt 14:29–32).

While Peter was focusing his attention on Jesus, he walked on the water, but as soon as he switched his focus to the sights and sounds of the storm, the wind and waves, he began to sink. We run into trouble, not only when we turn our attention from Jesus to things like our circumstances and other people, but when we look away to good things such as the baptism in the Holy Spirit, healing or the church. When we let *anything* else replace the centrality of Christ in our lives, we begin to sink. It is also very easy to put our trust in people rather than Jesus which can also land us in trouble. 'Cursed is the man who trusts in man' says Jeremiah (Jer 17:5), and no man can give you the ability to walk on water.

The temptations to put our trust in each other or in our own understanding seems to be particularly strong in marriage. A young couple marry and begin the voyage of their lives together, convinced that *their* marriage will never end in shipwreck! At first, everything goes well, but after a time the storm clouds begin to gather; problems emerge and grow more numerous. Eventually the storm breaks upon them in its full fury threatening to overwhelm them. The more they toil and strain to put things right, the worse they seem to get, until the only course open to them appears to be to abandon ship, and the divorce proceedings begin.

After a time, they may well repeat the whole process with new partners, convinced that they have learnt their lessons well, only to find the storms still raging not far from the shores of the sea of matrimony. It is a joy for me to counsel couples in this position, helping

IT'S THE GREATEST DAY YOU EVER LIVED

them to see Jesus in their storm, and to cry out to him for help. Then they begin to learn to walk on the water with him, no longer allowing their problems to dictate to them as Jesus becomes the Lord of their marriage. I know of many marriages that have been saved in this way.

There are many things in the world around us that would encourage us to turn our eyes away from Jesus and to put our trust in something else. Our television screens are constantly depicting people who are putting their trust in sex, money, power and lies. Adverts make claims which only Christ can fulfil. Some recent claims I have noticed include: 'Coke is it', 'Only Smarties have the answer', 'CU Life is for living', 'Sure, it won't let you down', 'Enjoy life with a regular monthly income', 'Standard life is for all of your life'.

You might think that if Jesus wanted to teach Peter to walk on water he could have at least picked a calm day for the first lesson! Or he could have rebuked the storm first and then got Peter out of the boat. Then Peter would at least have had a smooth surface to walk on, rather than the hills and valleys of the tossing waves. That was not Jesus' way; he wanted Peter to discover, by practical experience, that the best way of overcoming a stormy sea is to walk on it. We too can walk on our storms of life. Sometimes when I ask people how they are they reply, 'As well as can be expected, under the circumstances.' I then ask them what they are doing *under* their circumstances, and encourage them to believe that they could be living *above* them!.

Peter walked on water in response to Jesus' word 'Come' (Mt 14:29), and before he could respond in this way he had to recognise that Jesus was there with him in the storm. We have already seen that we can only walk on water by faith, and to do this we have to be 'looking unto Jesus, the author and finisher of our faith' (Heb 12:2). As we realise that Jesus is with us in the storm, and begin to look at him, faith rises, and we find that we are walking on water. Nothing can stop faith from finding its way to Jesus. When he first appeared on the scene during the storm on the lake, Peter thought he was seeing a ghost, but then he heard Jesus say, 'Be of good cheer! It is I; do not be afraid' (Mt 14:27). At that moment, fear left Peter and he discovered that 'faith comes from hearing, and hearing by the word of Christ' (Rom 10:17, NASB). If there was any doubt left in Peter, he dispelled it by his next remark, 'Lord, if it is you, command me to come to you on the water' (Mt 14:28). I call that an arrow prayer and I have found them to be so effective in an emergency, time and again. Jesus' futher word, 'Come,' was enough for Peter: he got out of the boat and stood on the water.

It is obvious to anyone looking at the matter dispassionately that the first step to walking on water is to step out of the boat, but that may be the hardest step of all. That boat does provide some measure of security in the storm. Maybe it will break up or be swamped at any minute, but while it is still afloat there is a chance that it will stay that way! The storm might pass if we can hold on for a few more minutes.

I do not know what security the boat represents in your life; maybe the medical treatment you are receiving will begin to work; maybe the other person in that relationship problem will change; maybe the employment situation will improve and you will get your old job back; maybe business will pick up and your accounts will soon be out of the red. The storm could be some sin in your life that you do not seem to be able to conquer however hard you try. You may feel that the best you can look forward to is a life of failure and condemnation as you struggle to contain that sin and pray that it will not swamp you. Remember that Jesus encountered that sin, but did not yield to the temptation, and if you begin to walk on the water with him, he will bring you to a place of victory over the sin.

You may reason that things cannot get much worse and that there is a good chance that if you sit tight and do nothing they will soon improve. A lot of people survive that way, but God does not want you to be merely a survivor, he wants you to be an overcomer, and that will never happen as long as you huddle in the boat. Change your survivor mentality today and take on an overcomer's attitude. 'Your attitude should be the same as that of Christ Jesus' (Phil 2:5, NIV) and he overcame death and hell 'and has sat down at the right hand of the throne of God' (Heb 12:2).

It is interesting to notice the sequence of events that resulted in Peter getting out of the boat and walking on the water. First Jesus gave the invitation 'Come' and Peter responded in obedience and faith to become a doer of the word. That is God's way of taking us on into new experiences with himself. Jesus did not give Peter a book entitled 'Seven Steps to Walking on the Water' and say 'Read this,' nor did he recommend a Bible College that has a special course on walking on the water. He did not even preach Peter a sermon or give him a set of instructions; he just said, 'Come.'

Now I have nothing against books and Bible Colleges, sermons and instructions, but at best they

HOW TO WALK ON WATER

can only help us to get to the place where we obey God's word and step out in faith.

When our children were learning to walk, Heather and I did all we could to encourage them. Their elder brothers and sisters and friends encouraged them to walk, demonstrating how they did it. None of us could actually teach them to walk; they had to do it for themselves by actually taking steps. They may have looked at people walking and thought that it looked very difficult and dangerous and decided that crawling on all fours was safer. Maybe they decided to postpone trying to balance on their two legs for a time and remain contented with crawling.

With our children, the breakthrough did not come when we gave them a lecture on the advantages of walking over crawling, but when we stood a short distance away from them, held out our hands and said, 'Come to me.' They responded by rising unsteadily to their feet, taking a few tottering steps forward, and collapsing in our arms. They had done it. They had actually walked across the floor! Exactly the same principles apply when it comes to walking in the Spirit, and when I speak of learning to walk on the water, I am really talking about learning to walk in the Spirit.

We cannot teach each other to walk in the Spirit. We can encourage each other, pray for each other and testify to our own experiences, but we each have to learn to walk in the Spirit for ourselves. I have several close friends with whom I have discussed walking in the Spirit, and I have discovered that we are all unique in our spiritual walk with God. If we tried to copy each other, we would only get confused and fail. There are no rules for walking in the Spirit, but there is one

IT'S THE GREATEST DAY YOU EVER LIVED

secret of success: faith. Walking on the water involves going where you have never been before and doing things you have never done before. You have no previous experience to guide you, and that of other people can only serve to encourage you that others have done it before and so can you now. A life of sticking to the old routines that you can repeat without trying may be safe, but compared with stepping out of the boat and into the unknown, it is boring. Life is exciting as you walk on the water, and those steps take you into the greatest day you have ever lived.

I will never forget the day that God called me out of my job into full-time service for him. I had quite a struggle getting out of the boat! I had a mortgage on my house, a hire purchase agreement on my car and several other regular financial commitments. I was earning good money but it was all committed when I got my pay cheque. I finally gave in my notice and made arrangements to take a team of eight on a mission in the Channel Islands. I have always been a team man and knew that this was the way I should start my new life as a full-time evangelist, but it was a big challenge to me. I told everyone on the team that I would let them have their expenses before we left England, which was another example of getting out of the boat and standing on the water.

My last day at work came to an end and I went to the office to get my last pay packet and my insurance stamp card. Then I said my goodbyes, got into my vehicle and drove out of the company's car park for the last time. As I did so, I sensed the devil whispering in my ear, 'Ha ha, now you're going to look a fool; where do you think your next week's wages are coming from?' I responded by beginning to sing a chorus and

HOW TO WALK ON WATER

then, as I drove around a corner, I saw a man standing at the side of the road. When he spotted me he waved me down and when I stopped he held out his hand saying, 'The Lord has told me to give you this.' It was a five-pound note, a very good day's wage at that time. I drove on saying, 'Take that, devil. Who else but God would pay me five pounds for two minutes' work?' I had begun to walk on the water, learning to live by faith with no visible means of support. I felt excited and exhilarated, and the feeling remains today. I have been living by faith now for over twenty-five years, walking on the water without sinking. There have been some fierce storms along the way, times when things were particularly difficult, but they have only taught me to trust God more.

I have had to 'walk on the water' in terms of my healing ministry too. Back trouble is one of the most common ailments in England today, and it it often accompanied by what is known as a short leg or a short arm. In fact, the skeleton is thrown out of alignment with the result that one arm or leg appears to be longer than the other. When I minister to someone with back trouble, I may get them to sit on a chair while I hold their legs out straight in front of them. If one leg appears to be longer than the other I pray and the skeleton comes back into symmetry, with the result that both legs now appear the same length. At the same time, the back condition is healed. Several years ago, at one of my Easter convention meetings, a guest speaker from the USA began to minister in this way. I had seen someone pray for a short leg to grow once before, but I was responsible for this conference so I felt very much involved and also conscious of my own lack of faith. Then I heard

IT'S THE GREATEST DAY YOU EVER LIVED

God whisper in my ear, 'I want you to move into that ministry and pray for people with short legs.' My first reaction was, 'No, Lord, I can't do that. Supposing the leg doesn't grow?'

A few days later, I flew to the USA myself, and went to Missouri where a businessman had arranged some meetings for me. On the Sunday morning he took me to a little country church in a very remote area. From the very outset of the meeting, there was a strong move of the Holy Spirit, and when the pastor gave the benediction, he said, 'I have to apologise to Brother Double. He came four thousand miles to visit us and he never got to preach.' It was true, the gifts of the Spirit had flowed in such a way that at no point had a message from myself seemed appropriate. However, that evening I did preach and moved on into ministering to the sick.

The very first person I prayed with had a bad back and a short leg, the first I had encountered since God told me he was bringing me into the ministry. The man had actually told me he had a bad back and a short leg, I responded by laying hands on him and praying. He crumpled into a heap on the floor and I moved on, conscious that I had not ministered to that man as God had wanted me to. I knew I had to get out of the boat and walk on the water, so at the close of the meeting, I went back to that man and asked him if I might pray with him again. In fear and trembling, I asked him to sit down and I took his legs. Sure enough, one appeared to be some three inches longer than the other. I began to pray, 'In the name of Jesus...' but before I got beyond the first five words the short leg shot out to the same length as the other. I was walking on the water and I have never had any desire to get back into that particular boat!

My colleague, Mike Darwood, was with me on this particular visit to the USA, and after God had dealt with me I wanted to see him out of the boat too and walking on the water in the ministry of praying for short legs. We travelled to Louisville, Kentucky, for some meetings in a big Pentecostal church and one evening a hundred or so responded to the invitation at the end of the message and came forward for prayer. I began to talk with someone who had a very deep problem, but after a time I saw out of the corner of my eye that Mike was talking to a woman over the other side of the church. I felt sure that the woman was suffering from back trouble and had a short leg, and afterwards Mike confirmed that this was the case. When he realised that she had a short leg, he tried to attract my attention in the hope that I would go over and pray for her, but I felt God restraining me from responding to him. In desperation, Mike sat the woman down and held out her legs to tell me what the situation was, thinking that I would be sure to take pity on him and go over to help him. I continued to talk to the person I was helping. Suddenly Mike realised that he had got out of the boat and had better start walking on the water! He prayed and that leg grew right before his eyes. Today, he prays for as many people with short legs as I do, with tremendous results.

That is how God got us out of the boat in the USA, but he is always seeking to get us out of one boat or another. One particular boat that many people have problems in leaving is in connection with the baptism in the Holy Spirit and speaking in tongues. They hear all the teaching on the subject and understand that

IT'S THE GREATEST DAY YOU EVER LIVED

many people pray in tongues as part of their personal prayer life. They know all about the scriptures, 'He who speaks in a tongue edifies himself' (1 Cor 14:4); 'And these signs will follow those who believe: In my name ... they will speak with new tongues' (Mk 16:17) 'And they were all filled with the Holy Spirit and began to speak with other tongues, as the Spirit gave them utterance' (Acts 2:4). They know that speaking in tongues in prayer will edify them. They know speaking in tongues can glorify God (Acts 2:11; 10:46). They know that on the day of Pentecost the disciples spoke in tongues and that Jesus himself said those who believe will speak in tongues. Yet when I pray with people like this, they so often just sit there waiting for something to happen. I have to tell them that it is no use them waiting for God. He is waiting for them to get out of the boat and start walking on the water. Like the disciples on the day of Pentecost, they have to open their mouths and speak; then they will find that the Holy Spirit enables them to speak in a language they have never heard. They will be speaking in mysteries in the Spirit (1 Cor 14:2). God will be glorified and they will be edified. As one ten-year-old boy put it, 'I talked nonsense and the Holy Spirit made sense of it.'

The same principle applies with those who are baptised in the Holy Spirit and speak in tongues, but have never prophesied, or had a word of knowledge, or interpreted a tongue in a meeting. They need to get out of the boat and begin to move in these other gifts as the Holy Spirit moves them on. I believe that many Spirit-filled Christians have never been used in some gifts because they sit firmly in the old boat saying, 'I speak in tongues, but God never uses me in prophecy, or gives me a word of knowledge, and anyway there are plenty of other people here that he does use in those ways.'

The apostle Paul exhorts us; 'Earnestly desire the best gifts' (1 Cor 12:31), and I firmly believe that the best gift in any situation is that which is most appropriate to meet the need at the moment. If someone is sick, there may be a gift of healing; if they are feeling depressed, a prophetic word of encouragement would be appropriate (1 Cor 14:3). As we walk on the water through the storms of life, constantly making ourselves available to the Holy Spirit, then we can believe that the scripture will be fulfilled in our lives that states, 'The same Spirit works all these things, distributing to each one individually as he wills' (1 Cor 12:11). I shall no longer be part of the problem, but will have become part of God's answer.

If you read through the book of Job, you will see that in Job 1:11 a storm began which raged for most of the book. By chapter 2 verse 7, Job's boat seems just about to sink, and his wife even advises him in so many words to jump out of the boat and drown when she says, 'Curse God and die' (Job 2:9). Job's response to the situation when the storm was raging and the boat seemed about to sink was to huddle in the bottom of that boat bemoaning his fate and blaming God for getting him into such a mess. This is a vivid way of paraphrasing the words of Job 2:8 'Job... went and sat in the ashpit' (JB).

For most of the book, Job and his friends sit huddled against the storm arguing about why it is raging, but it is not until God makes his voice heard above theirs, and Job responds in putting his own troubles on one side and praying for his friends, that any real change occurs. As the Bible puts it, 'The Lord restored Job's losses when he prayed for his friends' (Job 42:10). As Job began that prayer, he got out of the boat and began to walk on the water. As he did so, 'The Lord blessed the latter days of Job more than his beginning' (Job 42:12).

Like so many of us, Job had become problem-centred, and when we concentrate on our own problems they have a habit of attracting others, so we become bogged down in a raging sea of problems. As we hear Jesus calling us to get out of the boat and walk on the water, we move into a position where he can at the same time bless us and bless others through us.

Most of the sermons I have heard about Peter getting out of the boat put more emphasis on the fact that he began to sink when he looked away from Jesus than on the fact that he did walk on the water. The main lesson to be learnt from the sinking episode is that as soon as Peter realised what was happening he redeemed the situation by crying out, 'Lord, save me' (Mt 14:30). I am glad that Jesus did not wait until Peter was going down for the third time before he took action, but *immediately* he reached out his hand and drew Peter up to the surface so that they could walk back to the boat together.

When you get out of the boat to walk on the water, do not expect that you will get into trouble and begin to sink, but if that does happen, do not panic but call on Jesus to save you immediately and you will find that he is right there at your side, lifting you up.

When I travel overseas and am thousands of miles from my family and friends, it is a great comfort to know that Jesus is there with me and at the same time he is at home with my family. If any of us make a

HOW TO WALK ON WATER

mistake and get into trouble, he is there to get us out of it. Someone has said that he who never made a mistake never made anything, and we must never let fear of making a mistake prevent us from getting out of the boat. We must be willing to take that risk. When Peter got out of the boat and then began to sink, he found that with Jesus he was free to fail without being punished or taught a lesson he would not forget in a hurry. We may treat each other like that sometimes, but Jesus never does. He brings us out of the water, sets us back on our feet, and encourages us to walk again. As we look back on our lives, we can often see how our mistakes have become, in God's providence, stepping stones to success.

Some people make one big mistake and then develop a very negative attitude about their abilities, labelling themselves as a failure. They may take years to recover from their mistake, and some never do so, but Peter got up and walked back to the boat. As you read through the Acts of the Apostles, you will see that Peter got out of the boat and walked on the water a number of times. On the day of Pentecost, when all the disciples began to speak in tongues and nearly started a riot, it was Peter who stepped to the front and began to preach, without even five minutes, preparation time!

The result was that 3,000 people were saved. Only a few days later, at the Beautiful Gate of the temple, Peter got out of the boat again when he said to the lame man, 'Silver and gold I do not have, but what I do have I give you: In the name of Jesus Christ of Nazareth, rise up and walk' (Acts 3:6). The result this time was a notable miracle. You will find several other similar examples, particularly in the early chapters of the Acts of the Apostles. Every time Peter was able to get out of the boat and walk on the water, because he had learnt his first lesson well. As a consequence, God was continually able to use him in new and exciting ways. How are things with you?

If you stay in the boat, you will never walk on the water. If you get out of the boat, you will walk on the water, through the storm, into the greatest day you ever lived.

Throughout this chapter I have referred to various types of problems, temptations, situations and circumstances as the storms of life, and have used walking on the water as a picture of coming to Christ where he takes us through these things victoriously. However, I also believe that before the Lord Jesus Christ returns, people will literally walk on the water in Britain as part of the fulfilment of his promise that those who believe in him will do the works that he did when he was on earth (Jn 14;12).

We live in exciting days.

7. Fear Sees Ghosts—Faith Sees Jesus

The new Testament is hardly the place you would expect to find a ghost story, yet when the disciples were rowing across the lake after the feeding of the five thousand, they thought they saw a ghost walking across the water towards them. It was, of course, Jesus who was approaching them, but they did not recognise him. The Bible narrative describes the scene vividly: 'When the disciples saw [Jesus] walking on the lake, they were terrified. "It's a ghost," they said, and cried out in fear' (Mt 14:26, NIV).

Jesus had sent his disciples across the lake by themselves in the boat, while he stayed behind to pray. During the voyage, darkness fell and a storm arose which prevented the disciples from making any further headway and threatened to sink the boat. At that point, Jesus appeared on the scene; he came into view walking towards them across the water. You must admit that this was unusual; the disciples had never experienced anything like it before. It was unprecedented and unexpected and, as is so often the case in such situations, the disciples reacted in fear. If you have ever read a ghost story you will have noticed that it is all to do with fear: the one objective of the writer is to make the reader feel afraid. You could say that

IT'S THE GREATEST DAY YOU EVER LIVED

ghosts always produce fear, and of course fear produces ghosts.

The Bible tells us that not only were the disciples afraid, but they were also troubled. Have you ever been troubled by the storms of life when everything seems to be going against you, and you are unable to make any headway? Like the disciples you are struggling away for all you are worth and getting nowhere! All your plans are going wrong, you may be over your head in debt and you do not know which way to turn. That is a time when you are very likely to see ghosts—spectres of disaster, poverty, loneliness and all sorts of unpleasant things. You do not know that these bad things are going to happen and very often they never do, but fear whispers in your ear that they could. Soon after that you begin to see their shadowy forms stalking towards you through the storm.

Even good things begin to look like ghosts in these conditions. I remember the story of a soldier in the first world war who said that one night he was on sentry duty in the trenches, gazing out across no-man's land towards the enemy lines. He was troubled by the possibility of an enemy attack and afraid of what would happen if he failed to see them approaching in time. In front of him were some wooden posts with barbed wire entanglements festooned over them. These were really friendly things because they were hindrances to any enemy who tried to attack that particular section of the trench. While daylight lasted, he had seen the posts clearly and as darkness fell their shadowy forms still loomed before him. There was a little moonlight that night so the posts continued to be faintly visible, but as the hours passed those friendly shadows began to change into the dim outlines of

FEAR SEES GHOSTS—FAITH SEES JESUS

enemy soldiers, a ghostly, hostile army moving in to the attack! Fear produced the ghosts, which in turn produced more fear.

You could not imagine seeing anyone or anything more friendly and reassuring than Jesus, but to the fear-crazed disciples even he looked like a ghost. This is how the fear destroys your peace of mind and reduces you to a nervous wreck. It always concentrates on spurious, negative and trivial things and blows them up out of all proportion to reality. You begin to feel that you are not going to make it through the journey of life. Jesus is always there, close at hand as he was in the storm on the lake, but while the eye of faith will always discern him, fear sees only ghosts. Jesus himself becomes a threatening figure.

You might be excused for thinking that the disciples would have been full of faith so soon after the miracle of the feeding of the five thousand. They had not only been there, they had taken part in the distribution of the five loaves and two fishes that had satisfied that great crowd, and had even had a share of the feast! Mark 6:52 lets us into a secret; they had not really understood the lesson Jesus was trying to teach them through that miracle because their hearts were hardened. Hebrews 3:12 calls it 'an evil heart of unbelief'. This conditioned them to see ghosts and not Jesus. The phrase 'hard heart' or something similar is common in the Bible and a literal translation would be 'calloused heart'. You know what callouses are, those patches of hard skin that sometimes form on hands and feet. If you cut into the callous with a knife you will not feel any pain because it is insensitive, but if you cut through into the soft flesh beneath, you will find that to be tender enough!

IT'S THE GREATEST DAY YOU EVER LIVED

One way a calloused heart develops is through relating to miracles, rather than to the Lord. When the miracle takes place, we are full of joy and confidence, but only a matter of a few hours later we may be facing a storm where we desperately need to see the power of God at work again and it does not happen. Why? Because our relationship is with the miracle not the Lord. Some who have been healed by a miracle become sick again and seek further ministry for healing, but this time they stay sick and wonder why.

I remember one lady who came to me for help with her problem; there had been a time when she had had a deep walk with the Lord but this had now ceased. She said that sometimes when she went from one room in the house to another, she felt him going with her and when she had spoken to him, his presence was so real that it was just like having a conversation with a physical person. Now all that was in the past and she was longing to get back into that relationship. It seemed that no one could help her, and I was puzzled by the change until one day God showed me that she was relating to her past experiences and not to God. Her heart had become hard and calloused, and although Jesus was still there, she had become insensitive to his presence. His promise that he would never leave her or forsake her was as true as ever, but she was no longer living in the good of it.

Many Christians are famous for one special incident that occurred in their lives, one undoubted miracle they have experienced. Whenever they preach, testify, or even hold a casual conversation, this particular incident always features prominently. It seems that their confidence is based on it rather than the Lord, but it is already part of history and they would do better to leave it there and go on with God. We shall face each new day with confidence as long as we have an open, living, ongoing relationship with him. We shall recognise him in every situation in which we find ourselves, including the most violent of storms.

Early in my ministry, when I first began to travel by air, I was terrified of flying. Eventually I flew to Chicago in the USA, which was bad enough, but then came the prospect of flying back home. Shortly before the time of the flight, I was praying about the situation when God spoke to me very clearly saying, 'My Presence will go with you' (Exod 33:14). I received that as a personal promise and all the fear left me. I have never had any problems with flying since then, although I have travelled many thousands of miles by air. Once when I was coming home from Tanzania my plane was delayed at Nairobi, and after waiting for two hours we were told that one of the engines had developed an oil leak. However, twenty minutes after that, we were told that we could board. As we walked across the tarmac to the plane, we could see scaffolding around one of the jet engines and a group of men stood around shining torches on it and looking up at it. On the ground at their feet was a large pool of oil. It was not a reassuring scene, but God's presence was very real and I knew that he was going with me. I had an appointment to keep in England and I knew that God would see that I did so. I settled down in my seat and fell fast asleep, so great was my confidence in him.

We all get challenged by fear; only the 'super-spiritual' would deny that. The important thing is, how do we respond to that challenge? When the disciples mistook Jesus for a ghost, he said three things

IT'S THE GREATEST DAY YOU EVER LIVED

to them that will help us to make the right response, every time. Expressed in modern English, they are: Cheer up; it's me; don't be afraid.

I am told that the words 'fear not', 'do not be afraid', or something similar, occur 365 times in the Bible, once for every day of the year. I mentioned this one year at a New Year conference, and then remembered that we were in a leap year and the devil whispered in my ear, 'What happens on 29th February?' Immediately, I sent up one of those arrow prayers to God, asking him for an answer to the devil. God replied to my arrow prayer by saying, 'I will give you that day so that you can be an overcomer by faith.' I do not have to be afraid any day of the year, even on 29th February!

It is a good thing to go around confessing, 'I am an overcomer by faith.' Do you confess good things? Paul prayed that Philemon would become effectual or effective in the sharing of his faith by acknowledging every good thing that was his in Jesus Christ (Philem 6, AV). You have a lot of good things in you in him. Paul says they include 'every spiritual blessing in the heavenly places' (Eph 1:3), and Peter describes them as all we need for life and godliness (2 Pet 1:3). Confessing the good things that are in us in Christ puts our faith to work and it begins to function effectively both in our own lives and in our sharing of the gospel with others.

It is a great thing to make a daily inventory of some of the good things that are in us in Christ; there are so many of them that you can make a different short list every day of the year!

Unfortunately, many of us do just the opposite. We begin the day by making a mental list of some of the bad things that have happened to us and we confess

FEAR SEES GHOSTS—FAITH SEES JESUS

our fears and frustrations, our disappointments and failures. This ensures we begin the day thoroughly problem-centred and on course for another day of disasters. If we begin with a good confession, we start the day Christ-centred, headed for a feast of good things.

Job said, 'The thing I greatly feared has come upon me' (Job 3:25), and it is true that fear causes the thing we fear to come to pass. That has been called negative self-fulfilling prophecy. We confess that we believe something bad is going to happen and although we do not want it to, our very confession ensures that it will, because it is a spiritual law that we reap what we sow and that what we say is what we get. If we begin the day with a good confession of some of the good things that are in us in Christ, and keep thinking that way, when a storm blows up we shall be ready for it.

I remember the day when I came out of a meeting at the Albert Hall in London to find that my car, which I had left parked nearby, had been stolen. My reaction was to say, 'Thank you, Lord, I believe you want me to have a better car than the one I had. I believe that you will use this situation for good so that I get that car now.' Then for some reason I went on: 'I confess that I shall have a Rover 2000 by the end of the week.' That is exactly what happened.

As has been said before, the facts are less important than the way you react to them. All my wardrobe, apart from what I stood in, had been in the stolen car, but before I got up next morning, someone had been out and bought me some new underwear.

Remember that Paul told Philemon to acknowledge all good things that were his in Christ. Many people make the mistake of looking for the things they need

IT'S THE GREATEST DAY YOU EVER LIVED

outside of them, forgetting that they are already inside them in Christ. We do not ask God to give us these things, but we acknowledge that he has already given them to us as we say, 'Blessed be the God and Father of our Lord Jesus Christ, who has blessed us with every spiritual blessing in the heavenly places in Christ' (Eph 1:3). Then we receive by faith and enjoy them. If you confess at the start of each day that this is the greatest day you ever lived, then that will continue to be true when fear stalks around or when a storm blows up. If you begin the day with a negative confession, then by the end of the day you will have reaped the appropriate fruits and you will be able to look back on the worst day you can remember. However, if you start by confessing some of the good things that are in you in Christ, then you will reap the fruits of that confession, and as you climb into bed at the end of the day you will be able to say, 'Thank you, Jesus. That was the greatest day I ever lived—and tomorrow will be even better.'

Some people say that fear is a natural reaction when a storm blows and all you can see is a watery grave with ghosts haunting the scene as well. In such circumstances, they argue, a Christian has the right to feel afraid. The truth is that a Christian never has a right to feel afraid. As Jesus came to his disciples walking on the stormy water, he said, 'Do not be afraid' (Mt 14:27). This was a command, not a suggestion.

Later, when he had got into the boat, he upbraided them for having been afraid; it was a luxury they were not to indulge in! Do not let fear rob you of the good things God has in store for you today. When a storm comes, quote James 1:2 to it, saying, 'Count it all joy

FEAR SEES GHOSTS—FAITH SEES JESUS

when you fall into various trials.' Then raise your arms and welcome the storm saying, 'Hallelujah, Mr Storm, it is really good to meet you. I know you are going to be a blessing to me.' As you make that confession, you are sowing some good seed; you will feel better for it immediately and soon you will be reaping some good fruit into the bargain.

The second thing Jesus told the disciples to do was to cheer up. As you read the Gospels, you will notice that he often gave them a similar exhortation. Just picture the scene; there they were huddled at the oars in a sinking boat in the middle of a stormy lake with no hope of rescue, and up comes Jesus saying, 'Cheer up.' Once again it was a command, not a suggestion. Maybe the disciples found that hard to take and maybe you would react defensively in similar circumstances. Sometimes when I am counselling someone who is going through a tough time I will put my arm around their shoulder and say, 'I think this would be a good time for us to praise the Lord together.' Some might say that was being cruel, but I call it kindness. The last thing anyone wants in that situation is sloppy sentimental sympathy. There are a lot of people going around looking for that, but it never did anyone any good. Jesus was always compassionate to people in trouble, but he expressed it positively and lifted them up out of the trough so that they could rise above the storm and look down on it from their seat in heavenly places where all their spiritual blessings were waiting to be enjoyed (Eph 2:6).

Some people find it easy to say, 'Hallelujah, bless you, Jesus, praise the Lord,' when everything is going well for them, but if they cannot say the same things when a storm is raging and the boat is waterlogged,

IT'S THE GREATEST DAY YOU EVER LIVED

then there is something seriously wrong. Is Jesus more worthy of praise in a calm than he is in a storm? He is the same yesterday, today and for ever (Heb 13:8), so he is equally worthy of our praise and adoration whatever the circumstances. His loving kindness is always available to us and we can enjoy his company whatever is going on around us.

The two things that Jesus said that we have already considered—'Don't be afraid' and 'Cheer up'—were commands with the purpose of lifting them up into heavenly places. The third thing was a statement of fact: 'It is I', or literally, 'I am.' That was a reminder they needed, and as soon as it came I am sure their hearts began to beat faster again and hope began to return. Something good happened inside them. In the middle of a storm, it is important to remember that Jesus is always the 'I am', and nothing can alter the fact. He is never just the 'I was', or the 'I am going to be'. Whether you are facing a sudden storm in the immediate future, or a general stormy long-range forecast, that fact should carry you through each day. Whatever happens, the 'I am' will be right there with you, taking you through and providing you with everything you need from his inexhaustible supply of riches. You do not have to worry, because we only worry about the possibility of things happening that we do not want to happen but with Jesus there by your side, it does not matter what happens—the storm will never swamp you.

I love the old hymn that goes:

> Onward then and fear not,
> Children of the day,
> For His words shall never,
> Never pass away.

FEAR SEES GHOSTS—FAITH SEES JESUS

The fact that Jesus is the 'I am' all the time means that whatever happens he will be there to meet the situation with us, and we know that nothing could take him by surprise, or cause him any trouble. As you learn to see him in this way, in every and any circumstance, every day will be better than the last.

8. I'm a Blessing Everwhere I Go

There is a fascinating thumbnail sketch of life in the church at Jerusalem in its very early days, in Acts 4:32–37. The way that the disciples cared for each other and encouraged each other is illustrated by the way those who owned land or houses sold them and gave the proceeds to the apostles to be distributed to the needy as they saw fit. The passage does not say that they had no possessions, nor is it suggested that it is wrong for Christians to own property; however, possessions must always be held loosely so that they can be disposed of if God requires us to make the money available to be used elsewhere.

In particular, the passage introduces us to Joseph, a Levite from Cyprus. He obviously had a tender heart towards God and was quick to respond to an encouraging example. Soon he in turn was encouraging others, so much so that the apostles gave him a new name. We are all familiar with English surnames like Jackson, for instance, which tells us that someone was the son of a man named Jack, or names like Cooper and Smith which denote the trade followed by a man or his father. To Joseph, the apostles gave the surname Barnabas, which means 'son of encouragement'. It was as if they personified encouragement

IT'S THE GREATEST DAY YOU EVER LIVED

and said Joseph must be one of its children by the way he behaved. They could see the family likeness. This was no flash in the pan, because throughout the Acts of the Apostles, Barnabas is frequently mentioned, encouraging one person after another, including the apostle Paul. I believe that we should all follow Barnabas in being sons of encouragement.

When Barnabas invited Saul to join him at Antioch (Acts 11:25–26), he must have had some idea of his friend's potential, and by the time they set out together on their first missionary journey, Barnabas had probably seen that it would not be long before Saul eclipsed him. That of course, is what happened. In Acts 13:1 Barnabas heads the list of prophets and teachers while Paul (then still known as Saul) is last. By the time we get to Acts 13:43, we read of 'Paul and Barnabas'. John Mark accompanied them on that journey, but left them at Perga (Acts 13:13). When Paul and Barnabas were about to set off on their second missionary journey, Barnabas wanted to give John Mark a second chance, but Paul said 'no'. This led to a quarrel, and Paul took Silas while Barnabas went off with Mark. Barnabas' perseverance paid off, because Mark later wrote one of the Gospels, and Paul himself admitted, in Timothy 4:11, that Mark was useful to him in his ministry. In many different ways, Barnabas sets us an example in a ministry we are all called to exercise.

What kind of recent past record do you have as a son of encouragement? Equally important, how well do you receive encouragement from others? Some of us are very poor at responding to encouragement and often react by pouring cold water over the one who is trying to encourage us. One reason for this is because of our own bond of rejection, and where this is the case, we need to be set free to receive encouragement. Whatever the cause, if we find it hard to receive encouragement, we need to change, seeking ministry if necessary. We all need to be both able and willing to give and receive encouragement. Moreover, we should always have something to give: we should be sons of encouragement not just now and again, but whenever we meet someone who needs encouraging.

Sometimes selfish attitudes prevent us from effectively encouraging others. We should remember that our attitude should be the same as that of Christ Jesus (Phil 2:5, NIV) and that he himself said, 'It is more blessed to give than to receive' (Acts 20:35). The way that Paul and Silas responded to the problems they encountered in Philippi (Acts 16:16–40) illustrates the point well. They set a poor demon-possessed slave girl free and their reward was to be thrown into prison after first being flogged severely. If anyone ever had a right to complain, it was them! Yet we do not read that one word of complaint passed their lips. Instead, they prayed and praised God until he sent an earthquake that set them free. They were certainly a blessing to the jailor and his family, because they were all saved and I have no doubt that the other prisoners were also glad that Paul and Silas had joined them for a time.

I sometimes visit prisons, particularly Strangeways in Manchester, to speak to the inmates, and when I do so I am always challenged by the story of Paul and Silas at Philippi, as I consider the impact they made in the prison there under much more difficult circumstances than I face. However, I always go believing that God will make me a blessing there, and many prisoners have become Christians as a result of my visits. Of course it is much easier to believe that we are going to be a blessing in some situations that it is in others, but I do not believe that anywhere is too depressing and gloomy for us to exercise our ministry. God wants to use us to dispel the gloom and bring light and joy to the people we meet there. Remember, we are the light of the world (Mt 5:14). At one of my Easter conventions the Lord gave me a chorus that really caught on, and became the theme chorus of the whole convention. It went:

> I'm a blessing everywhere I go,
> I'm a blessing everywhere I go,
> With Christ in me, the world shall see
> I'm a blessing everywhere I go.

We need to have a vision for the fulfilment of this in our lives today. Therefore we need to have the compassion of Christ within us, flowing out to those we meet. This compassion, which is an expression of the love of Christ within us, is an essential part of our equipment for being a blessing everwhere we go.

At this point I should like to draw a distinction between the compassion Christ showed towards others and the human sentiment which is the best that many of us can aspire to. Far from building others up, this type of sympathy can be definitely harmful. Compassion lifts up; Jesus tells us that the Good Samaritan in the parable showed compassion towards the man who fell among thieves (Lk 10:33). I am sure that as the Samaritan bathed and dressed his wounds and then lifted him on to his donkey and took him to an inn, the victim felt profoundly grateful and encouraged. On the other hand, the human sympathy which commiserates without lifting up and moving on to a better place is actually depressive.

In these days when God is speaking about unity, we must be careful to avoid anything that causes division among us. Birds of a feather flock together, and while sympathy unites the sympathiser with the one receiving it, at the same time it tends to isolate them both from others who would take a more constructive view of that situation. They form a huddle that is sometimes called a 'pity party' and can be quite aggressive towards others they feel do not understand them.

Compassion draws its object into the loving care of the body of Christ. When Jesus had compassion on the crowds because they were harassed and helpless, they reminded him of sheep without a shepherd. He immediately prayed for men who would have the ministry of drawing them into the safety of the fold (Mt 9:35–38). In the same way, compassion should cause us to pray constructively for those we meet, according to their needs.

When we show this love and compassion in speech, prayer and action, we move into the power of the Holy Spirit. We can offer sympathy on a human level without any help from God, but his compassion motivates us to reach out in faith for a manifestation of the love and power of Jesus Christ.

It is possible for people to encourage others in a wrong direction; as Psalm 64:5 puts it, 'They encourage each other in evil plans' (NIV). For example, they might encourage each other to have their own way and do their own thing, to act independently of God and other Christians. They could also encourage each other to take the easy path, the way of least resistance. I do

IT'S THE GREATEST DAY YOU EVER LIVED

not find many people queueing up to take the hard path but there are many on the easy road, looking for the soft options. If I ever feel a bit rebellious and want to follow a certain course of action, even though I suspect that God may not want me to do so, I am susceptible to the sort of encouragement that says, 'Go on, God won't really mind if you do it.'

That is exactly how the serpent encouraged Eve to disobey God and eat the fruit of the tree of the knowledge of good and evil (Gen 3:1–5). That sort of encouragement may go on to say that what you want to do may not be in God's perfect will for you but that it could be in his permissive will (as far as he is concerned). It is true that he sometimes allows us to stray a little from his path without dealing with us severely, but we must never presume on his grace and mercy and think we shall always be able to get away with it. Let us beware lest we encourage anyone to do anything outside God's will.

The generation of Israelites who were led out of Egypt by Moses discovered this the hard way when they refused to go up into the Promised Land when God told them to do so. The story is told in full in Numbers 13 and 14 and summarised in Deuteronomy 1:26–46. God told the people that it was time to go up and possess the land, and twelve men, one from each tribe, had gone in advance to explore the countryside and report on what they found. The idea was that the explorers would encourage the people to go up and possess the land, but in fact ten of them encouraged people to rebel against God and not go up. Only Caleb and Joshua encouraged them to do the will of God saying, 'We should go up and take possession of the land, for we can certainly do it' (Num 13:30, NIV).

I'M A BLESSING EVERYWHERE I GO

They were saying in effect that whatever the cost, God's way is best in the long run—even if it costs everything.

Moses had been longing to lead the people into the Promised Land himself, but because of an act of disobedience, God told him he would only see it, he would not enter it. The job of leading the people would now fall on his assistant, Joshua. Twice in Deuteronomy (1:38 and 3:28) we are told that God instructed Moses to strengthen Joshua and encourage him in this work he was being prepared for.

It must have been hard for Moses to accept that Joshua would go beyond him and that his job now was to prepare another for a task he would have liked to do himself. However, Moses had sufficient strength of character to do that and do it well. I have seen several people that I had been training and encouraging go past me into a deeper ministry than my own. When we encourage others we must always be prepared for this to happen. We will only be able to do this if we are secure in our own relationship with God and in our ministry.

One way Barnabas encouraged others by his example was when he sold his piece of property and brought the proceeds to the apostles. We too should always be seeking to encourage others by example as well as in words. This means that we should be leaders in caring for others, alert to their needs and sensitive to respond at the right time. We should always be ready to receive a word of knowledge or a word of wisdom concerning the needs of others. When there is a job to be done, we should be the first to begin, encouraging others to follow us. Our attitude when we see a need should be to begin to meet it, saying to others around us by our actions, 'Come on, follow me, this is the way it is done.'

When I feel low and depressed, I am encouraged when I remember the Lord is 'my glory and the one who lifts up my head' (Ps 3:3). As I let those words affect me I begin to walk around with my head held high again and become the means by which God raises other drooping heads. That is a ministry to which we should all aspire, but too often we operate as pile drivers, pushing others further down. Kind, encouraging words lift others, but harsh, negative talk crushes them.

Paul exhorts us, in Ephesians (4:29)—'Do not let any unwholesome talk come out of your mouths, but only what is helpful for building others up according to their needs, that it may benefit those who listen' (NIV). The word 'unwholesome' could be used of a bad apple in a barrel; if it is left there it will affect other apples until they all become rotten. In the same way, some words bring doubt and unbelief into the lives of others, which can in turn lead to depression. It should always be our goal to bring the right word at the right time to build others up in their particular situation. We can only do that as we allow the Holy Spirit to guide us, giving us a word of wisdom or a word of knowledge for them when it is needed. This will happen more and more as we learn to 'walk by faith, not by sight' (2 Cor 5:7). Then our hearers will be 'nourished in the words of faith' (1 Tim 4:6).

We are usually careful to feed our bodies adequately, but we often forget that spiritual nourishment is equally important. Just as an undernourished body may become sick and even die, so we become sick within if we are not nourished by the words of faith.

I'M A BLESSING EVERYWHERE I GO

That leaves us in no fit condition to bring nourishment to others. We are more likely to feed them with negative talk which is like giving a sick person something that has gone bad, or at best junk food with no real nutritional value.

When we love someone we naturally want to help them and build them up, so that they can enter more fully into the blessings and provision of God. We would not mind even if they drew ahead of us spiritually as was the case with Barnabas and Paul. Jesus said that those we love should include our enemies. When they curse us or push us down, we should bless them and lift them up (Mt 5:43–44). We will continue to pray down God's blessing on them until they become our friends. If I hear that someone has been saying bad things about me, I often pray, 'Lord, bless them more than you bless me today.'

God told Abraham, 'Surely in blessing I will bless you' (Heb 6:14) and Jesus said, 'To everyone who has, more will be given, and he will have abundance; but from him who does not have, even what he has will be taken away' (Mt 25:29). In Romans 5:2 Paul speaks of 'this grace in which we stand'. As I read those words I picture myself standing before God with open arms to receive every good thing he had for me. As I do so, I find that it becomes easier and easier to receive yet more, but when I turn away from him, I have less and it becomes harder and harder to receive anything at all. Then I need to confess my dryness and repent of turning away from God, and move by faith back into the place of grace. As I stand there, I become equipped to become a blessing everywhere I go.

One day as Peter and John were on their way to the temple for a prayer meeting, they met a lame beggar at

IT'S THE GREATEST DAY YOU EVER LIVED

the gate. They never got to the temple, but more happened to them on the way than most of us ever experience in any prayer meeting! They must have been full of confidence that they were well equipped to be a blessing everywhere they went because when the beggar asked for alms, Peter replied, 'Look at us,' and when he had gained the man's full attention, he continued, 'Silver and gold I do not have, but what I do have I give you: In the name of Jesus Christ of Nazareth, rise up and walk' (Acts 3:3–6). Peter and John knew that all the provision of God's grace was available to flow from him, through them, to the beggar and they were such a blessing to him that he, who had been lame from birth, went into the temple' ...walking, leaping, and praising God' (Acts 3:8).

When Paul wrote to Timothy he testified, 'And the grace of our Lord was exceedingly abundant, with faith and love which are in Christ Jesus' (1 Tim 1:14). The availability of that abundant grace to the people Paul met depended on faith and love which are also available to us in Christ. The secret is 'faith expressing itself through love' (Gal 5:6, NIV). Our love for people and our longing to bless them motivates our faith 'for Christ's love compels us' (2 Cor 5:14, NIV) and we reach out in faith to receive from God on their behalf. We invest our faith and they reap a rich dividend. One reason why love is greater than faith (1 Cor 13:13) is because 'it is more blessed to give than to receive' (Acts 20:35).

I have a friend who, like myself, has an itinerant ministry and often stays in other people's homes. As soon as he arrives on a visit, he asks the family if they have any needs. If anyone is sick, he will pray for them to be healed; if anyone is down he will encourage

I'M A BLESSING EVERYWHERE I GO

them; if there are unpaid bills that cannot be met, he will make a contribution towards them. He is always looking for opportunities to serve and bless others. It is an example I endeavour to follow in my own travels.

The first time I stayed at the home of my colleague Mike Darwood, long before he joined the team, was way back in the sixties, when Mike and Muriel had only been Christians for a few months. We were holding a mission in their area and they offered us accommodation, although the whole concept of receiving from God and blessing others was new to them. It was the height of the strawberry season, we were in the middle of a strawberry growing area and I am very fond of strawberries!

However, to Mike and Muriel strawberries were an expensive luxury and they only had them once or twice during the season. That year, God so blessed them and us that we all had strawberries several times each week during the mission. God provided them in a variety of ways: sometimes we were presented with them as a gift and on other occasions we would open the front door and find a box of strawberries in the porch! This happened because I believed that like Abraham, wherever I went I should be blessed and be a blessing (Gen 12:2).

During a recent visit to Chile, my friend Bishop Ian Morrison introduced me to his aunt who was celebrating her hundredth birthday. She was a remarkable woman who was a great blessing to all her family and friends, even at that great age when many people would only be a burden. Each morning she was busy writing or painting and she blessed many in both these activites. During the afternoon, she had a siesta, but in the evening , she occupied herself in knitting for other members of the family. When the newspaper reporters visited her on her birthday they could only describe her as a ball of energy. She was determined to continue to be a blessing to all she met until the end of her life. And she was succeeding!

I had the privilege of knowing the late Harold Horton, a great apostle and pioneer of the Pentecostal movement, during his latter years. The last time I saw him was when he was in bed with his last illness. It was the time when the 'mods and rockers' conflict was in vogue among teenagers and I had with me a young man who had been the leader of a gang of rockers when he was converted in one of my meetings a few weeks previously. I wondered how Harold would react to this wild looking young man, but he just held out his hand and said, 'Hello, I understand that you know a very good friend of mine.' Seeing the surprised look on the visitor's face, Harold continued, 'His name is Jesus.' In this way, he bridged the generation gap. Harold had a habit of painting gospel texts and hanging them all over his home and after visiting the toilet the ex-rocker commented, 'They even have Jesus in the loo here.'

Depressed people are usually inward-looking, self-centred and constantly demanding attention from others. When I minister to that kind of person, I always endeavour to start them on the road to becoming a blessing everywhere they go. Taking the initial step in this direction can be a real turning point in their lives. Job spent a long time in the ash pit trying to get help from his friends, but the Bible tells us, 'The Lord restored Job's losses when he prayed for his friends. Indeed the Lord gave Job twice as much as he had before' (Job 42:10).

I'M A BLESSING EVERYWHERE I GO

You might at first find it difficult to believe that one of the most effective ways we can bless others is by confronting and admonishing them, but it is true. I might be troubled by a sin which was spoiling my life and harming those around me, and in that case what could be a greater blessing to me than to have someone lovingly confront me and lead me to repentance and a closer walk with the Lord Jesus Christ. Paul says, 'Brethren, if a man is overtaken in any trespass, you who are spiritual restore such a person in a spirit of gentleness, considering yourself lest you also be tempted' (Gal 6:1) and, 'Let the word of Christ dwell in you richly in all wisdom, teaching and admonishing one another in psalms and hymns and spiritual songs' (Col 3:16). The word 'admonish' in the above scripture is a translation of a Greek word *noutheteo*. Paul uses that word a number of times, and from it Jay Adams has coined the phrase nouthetic counselling.

He says that this confrontational approach should have the object of effecting personality and behavioural change through person-to-person verbal confrontation motivated by love, for the good of the person confronted and to God's glory. The goal of confrontation should always be to leave the person you confront with more of the life of Jesus and the fruit of the Spirit than they had before they met you.

I once did a Bible study on the 'one anothers' in the New Testament and found plenty of examples to study. They include:

"Exhort one another daily" (Heb 3:13).
"Let us consider how we may spur another on towards love and good deeds' (Heb 10:24, NIV).
"Teaching and admonishing one another" (Col 3:16).

IT'S THE GREATEST DAY YOU EVER LIVED

"Be kindly affectionate to one another with brotherly love, in honour giving preference to one another" (Rom 12:10).

These and other similar scriptures show a number of ways in which we can relate to one another and so be a blessing to one another. I would encourage you to do your own Bible study on the subject and then begin to put what you have learnt into practice.

One Sunday morning, not so long ago, on one of the rare occasions when I am able to attend my home church, I was prompted to arrive early and greet people at the door personally, telling them that God wanted them to know just how much he loved them. I reminded some that they were very special to God and told others that he accepted them. After that, we had a great meeting as the people begain to worship God out of a realisation of his kindness towards them and their appreciation of the fact.

In counselling, I am often approached by people who confess that there is little reality in their Christian lives. They go through the motions of doing what is expected of them, but it is all shallow and unreal. Our life springs from our union with God and the only way of improving the reality of our Christian walk is by getting closer to God. Jesus said, 'I am the vine, you are the branches. He who abides in me, and I in him, bears much fruit' (Jn 15:5). As others take some of that fruit and enjoy it, we are being a blessing to them, just by abiding in Jesus. At the same time, I have discovered that the very act of sharing the life that flows into me with others deepens my relationship with God still further and the flow increases. If you cut the flowers from a rose bush when they are full, you get a vigorous growth of the new buds that will in turn produce still more flowers, but if you leave the old flowers on the bush, that will reduce further flowering. In the same way, for example, if God shows me something exciting in my devotional reading and I share what I have received with others I meet during the day, then the revelation that I have received grows. If I do not share it, I soon forget it and the benefit is minimal.

As Christ lives in me in all his fullness, I experience in my life the reality of Romans 8:32—'He who did not spare his own Son, but delivered him up for us all, how shall he not with him also freely give us all things?' However, I am not to be a store house for these things but rather a distribution point where others can take them as they have need. We should always be looking for opportunities of serving others in practical ways. Every time we give someone a cup of tea or coffee we are fulfilling the spirit of Matthew 10:42, 'And whoever gives one of these little ones only a cup of cold water in the name of a disciple, assuredly, I say to you, he shall by no means lose his reward' (though most prefer their tea hot!)

I love to encourage people by inviting them to my home for a meal or taking them to a restaurant. I often do this with missionaries or local church leaders when I am ministering overseas. You might think it would be better to give the money in an offering, but I believe God is interested in people and enjoys watching those who have sacrificed so much enjoying a special treat. It gives me great joy, too, to bless them in this way.

Finally, if there is no one to encourage us when we need it, we can always encourage ourselves in God, as

IT'S THE GREATEST DAY YOU EVER LIVED

David did in the incident recorded in 1 Samuel 30:1–6. David had returned to his camp at Ziklag from an expedition, only to find that his own camp had been raided and the women and children taken into captivity. He certainly needed encouragement at that moment, but the best his men could do for him was to threaten to stone him to death. Then he strengthened and encouraged himself in God (v 6) and went on to retrieve the situation.

If your outlook today seems bleak and the future grim, be encouraged. Within the will of God for your life there is victory for you in the Lord Jesus Christ. Go up and possess the land—and encourage others to go with you.

9. Poverty Is Not a Virtue

Some time ago, on a quiz show, a competitor was asked what he would do to put the country right if he was the Prime Minister. He thought for a minute and then said that he would call in all the money and redistribute it evenly among all the people. He paused for a moment and then continued, 'And when I had spent my share, I would repeat the process.' While the story might make us smile, it does remind us that the problem of how wealth should be distributed is a thorny one and that opinions on the subject vary greatly, among Christians as well as others.

One prevalent attitude today is what I call 'lowest common denominator mentality'. Some look on poverty as a virtue and consider it to be a sin to have an abundance of anything! One thing is certain, Jesus wants us to have abundant life (Jn 10:10) and it is a mistake to confine that statement to spiritual issues only. On another occasion Jesus said, 'Peace I leave with you, my peace I give to you' (Jn 14:27) and I was interested to read the definition of peace given in the glossary of the *Translator's New Testament*. It said that in the majority of contexts the Greek word *eirene* (peace) is used in the Greek Old Testament (Septuagint) as the translation for the Hebrew word

IT'S THE GREATEST DAY YOU EVER LIVED

shalom and from which it was taken over into the New Testament.

It goes on to say:

> It [peace] contains the fundamental ideas of prosperity and well being. To wish a man 'peace' is to wish him every conceivable blessing from God, everything that will be for his present and ultimate good. This was the formal Hebrew greeting (Ruth 2:4).

Poverty is not a virtue, but part of the curse. As we read the first two chapters of Genesis, we find no hint of poverty in the Garden of Eden but find Adam enjoying God's provision in every area of his life. After his sin of rebellion in eating the fruit of the tree of the knowledge of good and evil he came under God's curse and from then on he found himself fighting for survival against a hostile world. That battle continues today and everyone of us is born into it. Praise God that at the cross Christ offers us deliverance from the curse.

The recent famines in various parts of the world, especially in Africa, have stirred many groups and individuals into action in attempts to help those who have been the worst affected. Powerful reporting by the media has aroused the interest of people everywhere and some of the relief schemes put into effect have caught the public imagination. Numerous visits to different parts of Africa have given me a deep concern for the people of that country and I am as anxious as anyone that they should receive the help they need. They are victims crying out for justice. The whole Bible testifies to the fact that God hates injustice and so must we.

Nevertheless, I am convinced that before rushing

into hasty action we should ask ourselves what is the right way to help and how can we best meet the needs of those affected by the famine? Ill-considered action, far from helping the victims, could do untold harm. It is essential that we seek God's guidance before we act in accordance with principles that are set out clearly in the Scriptures, as the Holy Spirit leads us. As I get more involved with Christians in third-world countries, it becomes increasingly clear to me that much sincere missionary effort has failed to produce the fruit that was intended and expected. It has proved to have been misdirected and the result has been an increase in atheistic communism, rather than the establishment of thriving Christian communities.

I have vivid memories of one visit to an evangelical mission station in Tanzania. The missionaries had established a school but this was now state-controlled and the curriculum for both boys and girls included military training. During my visit they were doing various drills and exercises and as they did so they chanted slogans of hatred including, 'Kill the white man, kill the Asian.' As a guest I stood on a platform and took the salute as the whole school paraded past me and they made a very impressive sight. The boy who had been trained to act as Sergeant Major issued his orders in a way that reminded me of my own military training; I am sure that he would have won the approval of any British counterpart! As the students marched along with impressive military precision, they were led by a band equipped with first-class instruments that had been provided and paid for by the missionary organisation. I have a permanent record of the event as I was able to film the parade.

IT'S THE GREATEST DAY YOU EVER LIVED

As I watched that day's events my heart sank. Something had gone very wrong indeed. Any attempt to meet the needs of people that fails to clearly represent the gospel of the Lord Jesus Christ will not produce fruit for the kingdom of God. To educate people in undeveloped areas without ensuring that firm Christian foundations are laid from the very beginning is extremely dangerous. Secular education alone cannot deal with the root problems of people.

When we become involved in relief work we must never forget God's law of sowing and reaping which operates in the lives of individuals and also of nations. I often say that if we do not like what we are reaping then we should change what we are sowing! A good example of this law in action is to be found in the first chapter of the book of Haggai. The prophet makes it clear to the people that they were reaping poverty and frustration because they were sowing seeds of selfishness and putting themselves before God. As a result, God's hand was against them, as Haggai 1:9–11 makes clear:

> "You looked for much, but indeed it came to little; and when you brought it home, I blew it away. Why?" says the Lord of hosts. "Because of my house that is in ruins, while every one of you runs to his own house. Therefore the heavens above you withhold the dew, and the earth withholds its fruit. For I called for a drought on the land and the mountains, on the grain and the new wine and the oil, on whatever the ground brings forth, on men and livestock, and on all the labour of your hands'.

It is clear that in this situation the people were not basically in need of financial loans, building projects or famine relief, but that they needed a real change of heart. Practical help given thoughtlessly could even have hindered that change from taking place! God was angry with his people and the famine and hard times they were enduring were a warning from him. Hebrews 12:5–6 seems an appropriate comment here: 'And you have forgotten the exhortation which speaks to you as to sons: "My son, do you not despise the chastening of the Lord, nor be discouraged when you are rebuked by him; for whom the Lord loves he chastens, and scourges every son whom he receives".' Verse 11 continues, 'Now no chastening seems to be joyful for the present, but grievous; nevertheless, afterwards it yields the peaceable fruit of righteousness to those who have been trained by it.'

In this instance, the discipline was effective; the people heeded Haggai's warning, repented and set to work to rebuild the house of the Lord, but if they had failed to do so they might have found themselves experiencing God's wrath and judgement. God is love, but let us not forget that he is also a God of judgement. He is total love all the time but he is also total wrath and judgement all the time. If we fail to include this truth in the gospel we preach, we are presenting a dangerously distorted view of God and are in danger of falling under the same condemnation as the prophets who said, 'Peace, peace! When there is no peace' (Jer 6:14). Haggai's words to the people were an expression of true kindness and proved to be very good news to them.

Although it does not appear that Haggai accompanied his warning with any practical relief work, I believe that acts of mercy to the poor and needy, whatever the reason for their condition, are compatible with the love and compassion of Christ. I once heard it put this way: 'We can always offer those in need a free sample of the love of Jesus.' If that ministry contains a supernatural element, then we will, at the same time, be offering them a free sample of his lordship too.

When Jesus healed the paralysed man at the pool of Bethseda (Jn 5:1–14), he did not preach him a sermon first but ministered to his physical need. That was a miracle, an awesome demonstration of his lordship and it was followed, at the right moment, by a warning; 'Sin no more, lest a worse thing come upon you' (Jn 5:14). I am quite sure the man knew what sin Jesus was referring to and that in these verses we have a good practical demonstration of the gospel, including both the love and the judgement of God.

Whenever we perform an act of mercy, either to an individual or to a nation, we should always be alert to the possibility that God may have something to show us concerning the situation. If he reveals that their condition is an example of sowing and reaping, a warning to them, or even part of an act of judgement, then we must be careful to ensure that anything we do makes it easier, not harder, for them to hear what he is saying to them.

Finally, we must remember that when people persistently ignore God's warnings, then his judgement may fall on them in a terrible way. There are numerous examples of this in the Bible, such as Noah's flood (Gen 6:1–8:19), Sodom and Gomorrah (Gen 18:16–19:29) and the sacking of Samaria by the Assyrians (2 Kings 17:5–24).

While it is easier to find individual acts of judgement in the New Testament, for example the case of Ananias and Sapphira (Acts 5:1–11), the principle of judgement

POVERTY IS NOT A VIRTUE

on communities is still discernible. For instance, take Christ's warning to the impenitent cities, Chorazin, Bethsaida and Capernaum, ending with the words, 'But I say to you that it shall be more tolerable for the land of Sodom in the day of judgment than for you' (Mt 11:24). This makes it clear that peoples are still subject to God's acts of judgement.

I am always disturbed when I hear people blame God for the suffering in the world, especially among children. I understand their concern, especially as they contrast the poverty in some areas with the high living standards, even opulence, in some Western countries. However, we must not forget that God has provided sufficient for everyone in the world, while man in his greed and the worship of economic science has produced food mountains in some countries while people starve in others. These unrighteous monuments remind us that man's lust and sin are causes of the world's problems. Even in Africa today some countries have good surpluses and are cutting down on agricultural production while across the border their neighbours are starving. The richer country may be sending military equipment over the border for political reasons, but not food!

When we preach the gospel of the kingdom, we must include redemption of the whole man, including the meeting of his physical needs. I have seen this happen with impressive results among some of the poorest people you could imagine in Africa and South America. The preaching of the gospel lifts people and that includes lifting them out of their poverty. For instance, some very poor people in South America have severe dental problems caused by their diet and the lack of dental facilities, even if they could afford to take advantage of them. I have seen God fill their teeth, in answer to prayer, with the most expensive types of filling used by dentists. Rex Gardner in his book *A Doctor Investigates Healing Miracles* devotes a whole chapter to this subject with convincing proof that it is happening, and I have seen examples of God's dentistry myself. I cannot explain why God is filling teeth in South America today, instead of healing them so they do not need to be filled, but I do rejoice that he is meeting the need.

As an example of preaching the Gospel to the poor in such a way as to lift them, I will describe a mission I conducted in a small settlement on the edge of a famine area in Africa. People travelled from near and far to attend, some walking up to seventy miles each way. As part of preaching the gospel of the kingdom, Good News Crusade financed the feeding of those attending, 800 in all, for a week. Some had not eaten a good meal for a long time. A field kitchen was set up and we made sure that as they fed on the word of God they were able to do so on full stomachs! They all had plenty of good food and the love of Christ was presented to them in a very practical way. Many were converted and baptised in the Holy Spirit and miracles of healing took place, including the opening of blind eyes. It was a joy to be awakened at 6.00 am each day by the noise of those who had assembled for prayer. I am sure that the daily feast they all shared that week was as much a part of the proclamation of the gospel of the kingdom as anything else that took place during the mission. We were putting the preaching of the word into its context.

One man I had the privilege of meeting in the heart of the African bush is a living example of what can happen when the gospel of the kingdom is preached as good news to the poor. When he was converted and baptised in the Holy Spirit, he was a poor peasant struggling to stay alive, but he was taught the principles of giving and began to bring his tithe to the church, a few cobs of corn and some eggs. He had nothing more to give, certainly no money. What happened next was an illustration of Luke 6:38—if you give, you will get. Your gift will return to you in full and overflowing measure, pressed down, shaken together, to make room for more, and running over. Whatever measure you use to give—large or small— will be used to measure what is given back to you. Soon he was bringing chickens and whole sacks of corn to the church and the more he gave, the more God gave back to him. It was the same principle of reaping and sowing in operation that I mentioned earlier in this chapter! The last time I had any news of him, he had a herd of 600 head of cattle, a large flock of poultry and an abundance of corn. He was still giving and giving and giving again, and God was continuing to give back to him, in full and overflowing measure, pressed down, shaken together to make room for more, and running over.

Another unforgettable highlight of my ministry is a visit I made to the Burundi refugee camp in Tanzania. Revival had broken out and some 16,000 out of a total of 50,000 refugees had become Christians. The meeting at which I spoke was held in the open air because there was no building on the camp large enough to hold the crowd. They had no expensive instruments to lead the praise and worship but music was provided by using Fanta bottles containing different amounts of water to produce the various notes. We all shared in

IT'S THE GREATEST DAY YOU EVER LIVED

communion, for which fifteen gallons of wine and three sacks of bread were provided. At the close of the meeting, about 10,000 sought God's healing power for their lives and many testified to being instantly healed.

One of the pastors told me how the Tanzanian government had introduced a scheme for growing tobacco at the camp which was in an ideal area for the crop. The Christians felt that it would be wrong for them to grow tobacco so they refused the offer and God had so blessed their other crops that they had not suffered at all. 'Come with me,' said the pastor, 'and I will show you how God has prospered us as we put our trust in him.' He led me to a church building housing some 3,000 bicycles. In that part of Africa, the bicycle is a status symbol that only the better paid such as school teachers can afford to own. God had certainly lifted the Christians in that Burundi refugee camp.

As we study the Scriptures we meet men like Abraham and Isaac whom God brought into covenant relationship with himself, which I understand to be a covenant of grace. These men became rich and God approved of their position; he called Abraham his friend (2 Chron 20:7). Then there is the example of Job who was the greatest of all the people of the East (Job 1:3). I have often wondered how many cars, Land Rovers, lorries and tractors a farming estate on that scale would have today. It is true that at one stage Job lost everthing, but let us not forget that God restored his fortunes and gave him twice as much as he had before.

The New Testament also has something to say to us on this subject. Take, for instance, 2 Corinthians 8:9—'For you to know the grace of our Lord Jesus

POVERTY IS NOT A VIRTUE

Christ, that though he was rich, yet for your sakes he became poor, that you through his poverty might become rich.' The Amplified Bible adds to the second word 'rich' the phrase 'abundantly supplied', which I take to mean having more than enough. I am aware that many Christians interpret this verse as applying to spiritual riches only, but we should be careful not to fall into the trap of supposing that because many people say something, it must be right. Jesus said the vast majority of people are on the broad road leading to hell, but that does not make it the right road to follow!

The Greek word for 'rich' *plousios*, and its derivative *plouteo*, appears in the New Testament thirty-eight times. In twenty-nine of these cases, the word obviously refers to material possessions, and in five more instances 'rich' describes an attribute such as mercy and faith or one's attitude to God. In Revelation 2:9, spiritual riches are contrasted with physical poverty, and in Revelation 3:18 material and spiritual riches are contrasted with each other. That only leaves the two examples in 2 Corinthians 8:9 and as the verse contains no qualifying phrases or references, I believe the word 'rich' there should be taken to include material possessions. Certainly Christ's poverty was material; no one has suggested that the verse implies that he became spiritually poor when he was on earth! The implied poverty of the Corinthians that was replaced by Christ's richness has to be material poverty in the context, so it seems reasonable to take the word 'rich' literally in this instance.

Moreover, the whole context of 2 Corinthians chapters 8 and 9 is the subject of giving material possessions, particularly money in offerings to other

IT'S THE GREATEST DAY YOU EVER LIVED

Christians who had less than the givers. The principle of sowing and reaping is again emphasised, as Paul says that those who give generously will receive back from God sufficient to meet their own needs and also have enough to give to others more generously than before.

To live in constant need is to live under the power of the curse; on the other hand trying to accumulate riches is displaying the big barns mentality of the rich fool in Jesus' parable (Lk 12:13–21). This is a dangerous policy as the story demonstrates. It encourages us to put our trust in our possessions instead of in God. To live in freedom from need with something always available to give to others, is to my mind genuine prosperity. When I live there, I can be a channel of blessing to others rather than a storage tank for my own benefit! The water in such a tank soon becomes stagnant and unwholesome so that it is of no use to me or anyone else.

Our prosperity should be measured by giving, not by our bank balance or our possessions. The Bible teaches tithing (Mal 3:10) but giving God a tenth of our income is only a start. If we withhold from giving both tithes and offerings we are robbing God and will feel the effects of the curse of poverty on our lives (Mal 3:8–9). I know businessmen who are so eager to finance others to take the gospel of the kingdom to their generation that they have launched out in faith to give far beyond the tithe of their income. Some give nine tenths and keep one tenth for themselves. That is a wholehearted, Christ-like attitude with no trace of selfishness apparent. It fulfils the spirit of Philippians 2:3–5:

POVERTY IS NOT A VIRTUE

> Let nothing be done through selfish ambition or conceit, but in lowliness of mind let each esteem others better than himself. Let each of you look out not only for his own interests, but also for the interests of others. Let this mind be in you which was also in Christ Jesus.

Then we have in Proverbs 11:24-25:

> There is one who scatters, yet increases more; and there is one who withholds more than is right, but it leads to poverty. The generous soul will be made rich, and he who waters will also be watered himself.

Generosity leads to blessing; the giver is refreshed and brings refreshment to others.

There is a great deal of emphasis among Christians today on the importance of ministering to the poor, the down-and-outs of society. However, there are others, who I call the 'up-and-outs' whose needs are just as great. Many have discovered that although money can buy them things, it cannot meet their needs. Only God can do that. In the course of my ministry, I have met wealthy people whose spiritual and emotional lives were in rags and tatters. It is also true that plenty of money does not ensure a trouble-free marriage, nor can it purchase physical or emotional health. We need those who can communicate with these wealthy problem cases and minister to them just as much as we need others with a ministry to the down-and-outs.

The principle of giving is fundamental to the gospel. Consider John 3:16, 'God so loved..., that he gave.' His gift to us of his Son Jesus to be our Saviour is an expression of his love for us. In the same way our love for each other shows that we have been born of God

IT'S THE GREATEST DAY YOU EVER LIVED

and know him (1 Jn 4:7). Giving to others should be an expression of our love just as it is with God. Consider your own giving over the past few months. If you were to measure your love by that gauge, how high a rating would you have?

Love that does not express itself by giving is suspect. 'But whoever has this world's goods, and sees his brother in need, and shuts up his heart from him, how does the love of God abide in him?' (1 Jn 3:17). Notice that John is speaking of our responsibility to our brother, not our neighbour. We do have to love our neighbour, as the parable of the Good Samaritan makes clear (Lk 10:25–37), but at a different level. The Samaritan ministered to the immediate need of his neighbour and in the same way, if I meet a tramp I might buy him a meal, give him some clothes, provide some medical attention for him, and in those ways I would be showing him the love of Christ. If my brother was in need, I would do as much for him as I would for the tramp, but beyond that I would be concerned to help him change *from being a net receiver to becoming a net contributor*. My goal would be to see him so prosperous that all his needs were met and he was able to meet the needs of others too.

James emphasises that love must express itself in action when he says, 'You see then that a man is justified by works, and not by faith only' (Jas 2:24). However, we have to face the fact that we British people tend to react when we are challenged to give to this extent. Somehow we become blind to the fact that giving is part of the gospel. I have heard some British Christians say that what I am talking about is American, but it really is basic Bible teaching. We will never move into prosperity and experience God meeting all our needs until we give in this way. I remember a very humble British pastor, Sid Purse from South Chard, say, 'If you are in debt and have no money, then give away the clock off the mantlepiece.' This will bring the law of giving and receiving into operation and God will meet your need.

Jesus says, 'Give, and it will be given to you' (Lk 6:38). Your gift will return to you in overflowing measure, pressed down together to make room for more and then running over. Whatever measure you use in your giving, large or small, God will use the same measure in returning to you. Recently I was ministering in a very poor quarter of a South American city when God told me to give someone 5,000 pesos. Within a minute of my doing so, an unknown local man handed me an identical gift. I was amazed, for this was a third-world situation of deep poverty. God's word operates everywhere, not just in the affluent West!

Every time we give we plant a seed. 'Do not be deceived, God is not mocked; for whatever a man sows, that he will also reap' (Gal 6:7). If you do not like what you are reaping, change what you're sowing. That is a basic secret of having a great day. If we are mean and stingy in our sowing we should not be surprised if God treats us in the same way. 'But this I say: He who sows sparingly will also reap sparingly, and he who sows bountifully will also reap bountifully' (2 Cor 9:6).

Giving out of one's need is a clear scriptural principle, although it has often been misunderstood. A good example of this teaching is to be found in 1 Kings 17:1–16. Read the story through and notice how God led the prophet Elijah to bring prosperity to the widow

IT'S THE GREATEST DAY YOU EVER LIVED

and her son in the midst of famine. When they met Elijah, their outlook was bleak indeed. They were about to use the last of the flour and oil to make a small cake. After eating this they would die of starvation because there would be absolutely nothing left.

Elijah challenged the widow to *first* make him a small cake which was something that, naturally speaking, she could not afford to give. Meeting his request would only hasten both her own death and that of her son. And what good would one small cake really be to the prophet?

Elijah's application of the principle of sowing and reaping seems hard, or even selfish, but when the widow baked him the cake, it brought God into her barrel of flour and her cruse of oil, and she could not exhaust God's supply. So Elijah's confidence in making her the promise that her supply of flour and oil would not fail while the famine continued was justified, and the three of them lived comfortably in God's miraculous provision for many days.

I like the statement, 'If God has his hand in your pocket, you can have yours in his.' When we live by faith, we are not living according to what we have but what God has. One hindrance to this kind of living, as we can appreciate from the story of Elijah and the widow, is fear. It grips us and brings us under the power of the curse of poverty. Fear leads to poverty. The widow learned she need not be afraid to give out of her need in a recession when it seemed that she could not afford to give anything. Whatever the situation, we should always apply God's principle of giving first. When we receive income we should tithe before using any of the money.

When I first began to tithe, I was already over-committed, with every penny of my income already spoken for. It was a real struggle to give the first tithe knowing I would only have nine tenths left to meet all my needs. It seemed that having paid the tithe I could not meet my commitments.

However, I can testify that God got into my accounts that day and from then on, the nine tenths have always gone further than the whole income did previously. I cannot explain how God's mathematics work, but they are more accurate than mine! Tight-fistedness is a big hindrance to receiving what we need from God. It may be that nothing will escape from a clenched fist, but nothing can get into it either.

Never allow your circumstances to dictate to you. I remember one occasion when I preached on prosperity with just a few pence in my pocket. I refused to let my circumstances influence my faith or dictate my preaching. At the end of the meeting, someone gave another minister who was there a new car! Live by faith not by your circumstances.

I have found giving to be an essential element of a great day. It is always my goal to be a net contributor. We should earn all we can and give all we can to enable others to share the gospel of the kingdom. I want to see the curse of poverty broken in the lives of others. As we contemplate the cross where Jesus became poor in order that we might become rich, we can release our faith to sow and reap.

I will never forget a man I met in the African bush, William Burton, a grand old apostle of the early twentieth century. He never owned a house or car, but he planted over 500 churches in his lifetime. He travelled round with all his possessions in one small case. I met him in Kenya and he told me he had to hurry to Nairobi Airport as he was to preach in Johannesburgh the next day. He had practically no possessions, but neither did he have any needs. Money was his servant to enable him to do the will of God. So should it be with all of us.

We will let the apostle John have the last word on the subject: 'Beloved, I pray that you may prosper in all things and be in health, just as your soul prospers' (3 Jn 2).

10. The Good Life

Today everyone seems to be preoccupied with averages. Is their income up to the average? Do they have as good a home as the average family, with the average number of children, motor cars, television sets and all the rest? You might see yourself as an average Christian, in which case it would be normal for you to have an average day and expect to live an average life.

That is certainly not how God sees you. His view is expressed in Ephesians 2:10—'We are God's work of art, created in Christ Jesus to live the good life as from the beginning he had meant us to live it' (JB). That 'good life' is nothing more or less than a succession of great days! Watchman Nee wrote a book entitled *The Normal Christian Life* but if you read it you will quickly discover that his normal is very far from average; it is a standard of excellence, an expression of the life of Christ through our own.

In 2 Timothy 2:20–21 (JB) Paul says,

> Not all the dishes in a large house are made of gold and silver; some are made of wood or earthenware: some are kept for special occasions and others are for ordinary purposes. Now, to avoid these faults that I am speaking

IT'S THE GREATEST DAY YOU EVER LIVED

about is the way for anyone to become a vessel for special occasions fit for the Master himself to use, and kept ready for any good work.

From a casual reading of verse 20 you might assume that just as some dishes are more valuable and more important than others, the same applies to us and maybe you are called to be an 'earthenware' Christian! A careful reading of the whole passage shows that the opposite is the case.

Nothing but pure gold is good enough for the King of kings and for his use. We are works of art, golden dishes, and to think less of ourselves is an insult to the Master. People who lead drab, sub-standard lives tend to sink into depression; God calls you to a standard of excellence and if you aim to live an average life you are aiming low. I was once speaking to a brother from a third-world country who said, 'In some societies the rich get richer and the poor get poorer; here we all get poorer.' That is the road to depression, but it is not God's way for you.

I do not believe it is God's will for any Christian ever to get depressed. In my own experience, when I have gone that way it is always as a result of some sinful attitude, behaviour or confession on my part. Depression does not just happen; it always has a root, such as an unwillingness to face the day when we wake up in the morning, or even a vague fear that something unpleasant might happen during the day. Then we are like the slothful man of Proverbs 22:13 who says, 'There is a lion outside! I shall be slain in the streets!' Although he was most unlikely to have such an experience, the possibility nevertheless depressed him!

THE GOOD LIFE

A few years ago, when I was preparing for my first visit to Chile, I got a fish bone stuck in my throat. It was very painful and eventually I had to have it removed by a minor operation in the local hospital, under a general anaesthetic. All this, on the eve of a challenging missionary journey, led to my getting into a negative, depressed mood and my wife, Heather, insisted I see the doctor. She pointed out that I was being very unpleasant to live with and she did not think that it was good for the family that I left them for three weeks overseas in that condition.

The doctor examined me and gave me a prescription, but it was not until I collected the tablets from a chemist that I realised they were anti-depressants. I have strong views on the use of these drugs and I said firmly, 'I am not taking them.' Heather replied, 'You either take them or snap out of it. You're not going to Chile in this condition.' Faced with those alternatives, I decided to snap out of it. I flushed the tablets down the toilet, and began to make a positive confession, trusting in the Lord for victory in the situation. There was an immediate change and I had no more trouble with that bout of depression.

In the Sermon on the Mount, Jesus told his disciples five times not to worry (Mt 6:25–34, NIV). Since he never makes impossible demands on us, this means that it is possible for us to choose not to worry, by an act of the will. A colleague has defined worry as 'unholy meditation', and another striking definition I have heard is 'negative thoughts whirling around a centre of fear'.

When I am counselling depressed people, it soon becomes clear that many of them are unaware of how much God loves them. This misunderstanding is the cause of much fear, anxiety and depression, as it is the love of God that drives fear from our lives. John tells us that 'perfect love casts out fear, because fear involves torment. But he who fears has not been made perfect in love' (1 Jn 4:18). That love is available to us as Christians, 'because the love of God has been poured out in our hearts by the Holy Spirit who was given to us' (Rom 5:5).

You can only trust someone fully when you know that they love you so much that they will never let you down. God is like that. The Bible often speaks of his lovingkindness and the wonderful thing about that love is that it is in no way dependent upon us, but totally to do with God himself. 'God demonstrates his own love towards us, in that while we were still sinners, Christ died for us' (Rom 5:8).

When we feel that someone we love has let us down, our relationship with them is affected and the bridge of trust between us has to be rebuilt. Jesus never lets us down: 'If we are faithless, he remains faithful; he cannot deny himself' (2 Tim 2:13). Therefore we can rest secure in the knowledge that God is for us and will deal with anything that comes against us. Nothing can drive a wedge between us and his love.

> For I am persuaded that neither death nor life, nor angels nor principalities nor powers, nor things present nor things to come, nor height nor depth, nor any other created thing, shall be able to separate us from the love of God which is in Christ Jesus our Lord (Rom 8:38–39).

An inferiority complex can be a very powerful force in our lives, causing havoc with our feelings and robbing us of the many blessings that God is longing to pour out on us. I used to have an enormous inferiority complex and I was quite proud of it, because far from seeing it as a bondage on my life, I thought it was a virtue, a sign of my humility! Then one day at a meeting, God spoke to me about it through a word of knowledge, telling me that he wanted to set me free from it.

When I recovered from my surprise, I responded and God set me free, showing me that I never need feel inferior again. The Holy Spirit in me is just as good as in anyone else and he gives me the ability to do all that God requires of me. This includes being a good father and husband as well as a good and faithful worker. The same is true for you. Depression often makes us feel that we are inferior to everyone else, and the odd man out in any company. The truth is that 'his divine power has given us everything we need for life and godliness through our knowledge of him who called us by his own glory and goodness' (2 Pet 1:3, NIV).

Many of us can look back to a past of failures and defeats, but if we look to the word of God, we read, 'If anyone is in Christ, he is a new creation; old things have passed away; behold, all things have become new' (2 Cor 5:17). God is a master craftsman and when he made this world and everything in it, he saw that it was all 'very good' (Gen 1:31). He did not lower his standard when he made you a new creature. You are not second-class material and there is nothing inferior about you. Therefore we can lay aside those negative thoughts about our abilities to be what he calls us to be and lift our heads high as we think about the One who made us.

We need to develop the habit of making a positive

confession based on the word of God and this often begins with a confrontation of our own self-rejection. When we write ourselves off as a failure, we are criticising God's workmanship (Eph 2:10) and that is a sin we need to repent of. We have seen that when Job thought about all that had happened to him, how he had lost his family, possessions and health, he 'went and sat in the ashpit' (Job 2:8, JB). Now the ash-pit is a place where we throw rubbish, things that are of no further use and when Job went there, he was classifying himself as rubbish!

Note too that he chose to go there, neither God nor Satan put him there. When I speak on this subject, I sometimes ask my congregation if any of them have ever been in the ash-pit and I always get a positive response!

Whenever we think about getting into the ash-pit, we should stop and remind ourselves what God says about us. For example, you might say, 'The word of God tells me that I am his work of art (Eph 2:10 JB). I agree with you, God, I am your work of art, and the ash-pit is no place for me.' This is not a case of mind over matter, but of being 'transformed by the renewing of your mind' (Rom 12:2). As this change takes place we are no longer negative, depressed, discouraged and defeated. Paul says, 'Your attitude should be the same as that of Christ Jesus' (Phil 2:5, NIV). We can ask him to let us see ourselves as he sees us and adopt his own attitude towards ourselves.

Paul prayed for his friend Philemon 'that the communication of thy faith may become effectual by the acknowledging of every good thing which is in you in Christ Jesus' (Philem 6, AV). We must communicate our faith and not shut ourselves away in

THE GOOD LIFE

our own little world. When I counsel a depressed person, I often find myself coaxing them out of the hideaway into which they have retreated. They usually begin to emerge by sharing with me something quite trivial in itself, a surface issue maybe, but very important to them at the time and not easy for them to share. I always take what they say seriously and deal with it thoroughly. They may share several of these secondary problems in turn and although I am not deceived and am aware that we have not yet got down to the real issues, I continue to deal with the problems they raise.

As we go on in this way, they slowly gain confidence in me and come further and further out of their shell and eventually we come to the real issues in their life, the things that drove them into a corner in the first place, and these can be dealt with once and for all. This process may take several chats together as the person concerned and I slowly build a bridge of trust between us. When it is strong enough, I can cross over it and help them.

When they really begin to trust me, I teach them how to communicate their faith by acknowledging all the good things that are in them in Christ Jesus. The gospel is good news and all the good things it includes are available to us. You can begin this acknowledgement by confessing 'Christ in me' several times a day, but especially first thing in the morning when you wake up. Then go on to begin confessing the good things that are in you in him. It will take you a lifetime to complete the list, but there is a useful short list of good things that you could start with.

'Thanks be to God, who gives us the victory through our Lord Jesus Christ' (1 Cor 15:57).

IT'S THE GREATEST DAY YOU EVER LIVED

'Yet in all things we are more than conquerors through him who loved us' (Rom 8:37).

'Now thanks be to God who always leads us in triumph in Christ' (2 Cor 2:14).

'God abides in us, and his love has been perfected in us' (1 Jn 4:12).

'It is because of him that you are in Christ Jesus, who has become for us wisdom from God—that is, our righteousness, holiness and redemption' (1 Cor 1:30, NIV).

'For God has not given us a spirit of fear, but of power and of love and of a sound mind' (2 Tim 1:7).

As you begin to confess these Bible truths, you will soon discover that your negative attitudes are going as you adopt the same attitudes as those of Christ Jesus (Phil 2:5). You may find it helpful to have someone else listen as you say these verses aloud, to check that you are not missing out any of the good things on your list. Also, the very act of sharing them with someone else does something good for us and helps them to become part of our thinking.

On one occasion, when Jesus and his disciples were crossing the lake, a great storm arose, so that even those experienced fishermen were afraid and thought they were lost. Jesus was asleep at the time so they woke him and asked him to save them. In response, he got up and spoke to the wind and waves saying to the sea, 'Peace, be still' (Mk 4:39). I like the way Jesus spoke to the situation and changed it. So often we accept our circumstances and settle down in them, letting them produce depression in us. We say, 'Because this happened, it must be God's will for me.' The disciples were saying to Jesus, in effect, when they woke him: 'You told us to cross the lake, but we

THE GOOD LIFE

are having problems because of our circumstances. We need your help to complete the job you gave us to do.' Jesus responded immediately and modified the circumstances so that they could obey him.

We too can call on him in this way and we can also begin to speak to our circumstances ourselves, in his name, in accordance with his word.

There is, however, another side to this coin because Scripture tells us 'And we know that all things work together for good to those who love God, to those who are the called according to his purpose' (Rom 8:28). So we can expect our circumstances to do us good, however hostile they may appear, but note that for this to happen three conditions have to be observed:

Firstly, we have to love God.

Secondly, we have to be called according to his purpose, and fully committed to his plan for our lives. For the disciples, at the time the storm arose, God's plan for their lives was that they should cross the lake, and as they sailed on they were endeavouring to fulfil that plan. In the same way, we should always be working with God for the fulfilment of his plans for our lives.

Thirdly, we have to *know* that all things are working together for good. If we do not know it, then it may not be happening. Personal knowledge of this fact is essential for us to live in the good of this verse.

I am quite sure that when the storm broke, it seemed to the discipes that things were going wrong. It is at this very point, when the situation seems to be getting out of hand and preventing us from doing what we believe God has called us to do, that we need to confess that all things are working together for good. That is the time to remember that he who is the

Alpha and Omega, the beginning and the end, is in control. He is for you and he loves you and he can be trusted to be working for your good at this very moment. Even if you cannot see him at work in this way, you can know that he is, because he has promised that he will. We have his guarantee from his word, and we can believe it in the face of all the evidence to the contrary. This is not indulging in wishful thinking; it is just agreeing with God!

There is an old chorus which includes the line: 'Feelings are not facts, but upon the word of God I stand.' If you allow your feelings to dictate to you, then you will always be vulnerable to negative happenings such as unexpected storms on the lake, or an unexpected bill through the letterbox. Maybe a friend has forgotten your birthday, or forgotten a promise he made you. All sorts of things can constitute a storm on the lake, and if at that moment we allow feelings to dictate to us we shall start looking around for an ash-pit to sit in! Rather than let our feelings dictate to us we should come to the place in faith where they are firmly under our control. Here are five steps we can take in coming to that place:

Step One

Discover what God's word has to say on the situation in which you find yourself.

Step Two

Accept that word, believe it, and confess what it says.

Step Three

Receive what God's word says, in your faith.

Step Four

Praise God for what he says, because praise is a natural attribute of faith. God's word commands us: 'In everything give thanks; for this is the will of God in Christ Jesus for you' (1 Thess 5:18). It is vital that we praise God in spite of our circumstances if we are to live in his victory. We can always praise God if for no other reason than he is worthy of our praise (Rev 5:12) and there is no better reason for doing so. Praise is therapeutic. Psalm 22:3 says, 'But you are holy, who inhabit the praises of Israel' and when we praise him, we are in the presence of the Great Physician himself who will bring us healing. He is also the King of kings who always has the last word in every situation. We can praise him, knowing that word will be for our good.

Step Five

Let your feelings come into line with your faith.

My colleague, Mike Darwood, tells of a journey he once made from Penzance in the far west of Cornwall to Carlisle in the far north of England. He left Penzance late one evening, slept for a few hours at his home in St Austell, and then went on with the journey which had to be completed by that afternoon. This was before there was a motorway from Exeter to Carlisle and, as the sun came up, all Mike could see was the prospect of a long, tiring and frustrating journey. Everything seemed to be working together for his discomfort, and he said to Muriel, 'We are in for a long hard journey and we will both be tired out when we get there.' Muriel agreed, and then they both realised that by their negative confession, they were signing a delivery note from Satan for the very thing they were dreading! They knew they were making the journey in the will of God, so they could be confident that he would cause all things to work together for their good and see that they arrived at their destination safely. They confessed all this, received it in their faith, praised God all the way, and arrived safely in good time and in good condition to serve God when they got there.

On another occasion I needed a new car, so I went to my garage to order it, only to be told that the workers at the factory were on strike and there was a long waiting list for orders. As in addition to all this I had no money to buy the car, things looked black. Then I attended a meeting where Colin Urquhart was speaking on the subject 'Anything You Ask'. I believed what I heard and received my new car by faith. Then I began to confess that it would be delivered by May 1st—in about three weeks' time. According to my garage, the earliest time I could expect delivery was the autumn. The salesman had phoned all his likely contacts to see if anyone could help me but all the replies were negative.

Twenty-four hours after I had heard Colin speaking and had received my car by faith, my garage phoned up to say that one of their customers had cancelled his order for a car—exactly the one I had ordered! I praised God as I went to collect my car on May 1st, since God had not only provided the car but also the money with which to pay for it. We have an old saying on my

THE GOOD LIFE

team: 'God always provides on time, though sometimes he cuts it mighty fine!'

Sometimes the gap between our confession of what we believe God will do and evidence that he is doing it can be very challenging. Here we can take a lesson from Sarah, Abraham's wife. When God told her she was to have a child she was already past child-bearing age, having been barren all her life, and at first there was no evidence that she was pregnant.

Hebrews 11:11 tells us how she handled the situation: 'By faith Sarah herself also received strength to conceive seed, and she bore a child when she was past the age, because she judged him faithful who had promised.' This is an expression of a tremendous attitude of faith. God had spoken and Sarah knew that his word could be trusted. It could not fail, however long she had to wait for its fulfilment, or however impossible the circumstances. So she never gave up, even though she did have to wait.

God had first spoken to her husband Abraham when he was seventy-five years old, telling him that from his offspring, God would make a great nation (see Genesis 12:2,4). The birth of Isaac was the beginning of the fulfilment of that promise and this did not occur until Abraham was 100 years old. Naturally speaking, the promise was impossible to fulfil because Sarah had experienced the change of life, but that did not stop her believing. Neither was Abraham's faith affected: 'He did not waver at the promise of God through unbelief, but was strengthened in faith, giving glory to God' (Rom 4:20). Husband and wife shared a common faith and confession and refused to let the time gap rob them. They judged God faithful and so he proved to be.

IT'S THE GREATEST DAY YOU EVER LIVED

Hannah (1 Sam 1) is another Old Testament character who was not affected by a time gap. She too was longing for a child although there was a general consensus of opinion that her barrenness was God's will for her. She became very depressed, and showed all the classic symptoms of that condition: loss of appetite, weeping, sadness and deep distress. She described herself to Eli the priest as desperate, troubled and miserable. After he had prayed with her and assured her that God would grant her request, her symptoms left her and she was at peace, although it was not until she had returned home that she became pregnant.

When one of my colleagues joined my team he began to suffer from painful haemorrhoids and although several of us prayed for him, the condition kept getting worse. He considered going to his doctor, but on that occasion he plainly heard God say, 'No, I do not want you to go to the doctor this time. I am going to heal you myself.' From then on, he sought ministry for healing, but it was just a year after the start of the condition when it happened. He went to a meeting where two young men prayed for him and he was instantly healed. He had heard from God and the time gap did not prevent him from receiving the fulfilment of the promise.

*   *   *

Today, and all the coming days that the Lord gives us on earth, can be great days. Ask him to make today one of them. He has promised to give good things to those who ask him (Mt 7:11). You will be asking for a

THE GOOD LIFE

good thing if you ask God to make today the greatest day you ever lived.

We can be sure that God is for us, and that he will deal with anything that is against us. He loves us and wants the best for us. He wants every today to be a great day.